The Miracle of the Universe

Where do I stand...?

Reflections by

Fr. Christopher Fox, M.H.M.

Christopher Fox

First published in Ireland, in 2021, in co-operation with
Choice Publishing, Drogheda, Co. Louth, Republic of Ireland.
www.choicepublishing.ie

ISBN: 978-1-913275-39-6

I dedicate this book to all who seek the truth with sincerity and an open mind.

I search and seek I know not what,
I only know it must be there,
For in my heart there is a quest
For something more than earth lays bare.

For even in the midst of bliss
Or what for bliss does falsely pass
I know there's something hid from me
Some truth beyond this earthly mass.

And so I delve and probe and sift
The sands on this our exile shore
To find that dim elusive truth
That stands when time shall be no more.

Contents

Introduction

The Greek philosopher Socrates once said that the unexamined life is not worth living. As I approach my ninetieth birthday it is a good time to look back over the years and the changes in my own life and in the Church and how these affect one's journey through life.

I grew up in the thirties and forties in rural Ireland. My parents were devout Catholics and obviously their influence was paramount in shaping my formation. We got by on a modest farm but we all had to play our part in the many chores entailed. I still have vivid memories of picking potatoes on a cold morning with numbing fingers. There was a good community spirit. Neighbours would drop by in the evening and exchange local gossip. Newspapers were rarely seen. The family rosary was routine. There was no crime. We never locked the door of the house when we went to Mass on Sunday

Religion came to us clothed in the garments of penance. Preparation for First Holy Communion and for Confirmation was not a joyful experience with too much emphasis on obligation rather than celebration, with fear of God more stressed than love of God. Later on when studying moral theology in the Seminary sin and obligation were dominant factors. The multiplication of mortal and venial sins would do justice to any rigid Pharisee.

As a young priest I greatly welcomed the changes that took place after the second Vatican Council. We discovered the spirituality of Easter, the goodness of all creation and the importance of secular values. We added the 15th station, the Resurrection, to the way of the Cross. Black vestments were left in the drawer. *Dies Irae,* a hymn about the wrathful judgement of God was heard no more. Many imposed penances were removed to give people more responsibility about what was suitable for them. The good news of the Gospel was emphasised. In prayer we were encouraged to make the longest journey, from the head to the heart. Revelation was seen not just as God revealing to us what to believe and how to act, but rather as communion with a loving God sharing divine life with us. Faith was understood not just as intellectual belief in God but should be experienced as a loving trust in God whom we dare to call Abba, Father.

As I write these words, early in 2021 with corona-virus dominant the future looks challenging for society as a whole and for the Church. What is God saying to us by this epidemic? For some it is a sign that God does not exist. For many it is a reminder how dependent we are on circumstances beyond our control. Thank God medical science is making good progress fighting the disease but it will take a long time.

How will the Church fare when it is all over? It is very hard to predict. In addition to facing up to the challenge of getting people to attend church regularly, it has to bear the burden of past scandals, such as clerical sexual abuse and more recently the mother and child revelations when unmarried mothers and their babies were treated in a most unchristian way and so many babies were left to die without care and buried in unmarked graves. Unmarried mothers were denounced from the altar. Reading about that whole scandal now fills me with anger and revulsion.

Yet I believe that the Church will be saved by good women and men, by dedicated priests and religious and by courageous leadership. It will be purified and chastened by this desert experience and we should remember that it was in the desert that God revealed Himself to the Israelites, purified them and made them His people.

Chapter One

The Amazing Universe

Did you ever reflect on the mystery of the universe? I sometimes ask people: is the universe infinite? If not, then what's outside it? New discoveries by the Hubble telescope give us some incredible facts to ponder. The universe is thought to have been created by a vast explosion (the Big Bang) between ten and fifteen billion years ago. All the matter that exists was formed in a fraction of a second in a tiny small space, at the same time bursting outward at incredible high speed. With this expansion, the matter flung out began to cool and over time the universe as we know it was formed.

Five billion years ago, the solar system existed only as a cloud of dust and gas. A mighty explosion took place and through an incredible series of reactions, the Milky Way, including our sun, was formed. The inner planets, including Mercury, Venus, Earth and Mars were formed close to the sun. Then came the giant planets, Jupiter, Saturn, Uranus and Neptune. Then followed Pluto and a stream of asteroids and comets. The complexity of it all just boggles the mind.

Each one of us is but a tiny speck of life existing for a moment of time on planet Earth. This in turn is but a small dot in the Milky Way which in turn is but a fraction of the universe. At the core of some galaxies there are black holes capable of swallowing up two million of our suns. And yet we believe that a loving Creator is behind it all and that each one of us is important.

I need to read again God's message to the prophet Jeremiah... *"Before I formed you in the womb I knew you, before you came to birth I consecrated you"*.

Each one of us is precious in the mind of God, whose Son lived among us and died on the Cross for our salvation. God created all things. The mysteries of the universe reflect the power and glory of the Creator. We join with all creation in a hymn of praise to God.

A Song of Praise
(inspired by the new discoveries of the Hubble telescope)

All you towering thunderheads, ten trillion kilometres high,
All you mighty nuclear fires, seven thousand light years from earth,
All you mighty nebulae, Eagle, Catseye, a million others,
radiating colour, beauty, power and wonder
Give glory and eternal praise to God.

And you mighty cartwheel galaxy, bashed out of shape
by a shooting monster. And you giant constellation Draco
and you, Eta Corinae, you mighty star, 150 times our sun,
four million times as bright, ten thousand light years from earth
Give glory and eternal praise to God.

And you, gigantic black holes at the core of the galaxies
that can swallow up two million of our suns
fifty million light years from the earth.
And you mighty quasers, stars, constellations, black holes
Give glory and eternal praise to God

And me too, in my puny little existence, yet with intellect and will,
Created in the image and likeness of God,
With the capacity to ponder with awe and reverence
The incredible universe around us, let me too, with all creation,
Give glory and eternal praise to God.

Chapter Two

The mystery of God

As we go through life we are confronted with many questions. Has life any meaning at all? We experience happy events, a good job perhaps, a lovable partner, sporting success and many celebrations. Yet we are involved in a world where there are many tragic events, a tsunami wiping out many people, a serious accident to some of our friends, the early death of a dear one and now this dreadful corona-virus. Why do these things happen? Has life any meaning or is it just *"a tale told by an idiot, full of sound and fury, signifying nothing?"* Are we all alone in this great universe? Does death put an end to everything for me? For many it often seems to be so. We live out our days in uncertainty. So let us eat, drink and be merry for soon we will be dead and forgotten.

Yet no! Deep within us there is a strong feeling that life has a meaning, that it has a purpose, however obscure that purpose may be. We are often caught between the confusion around us and the conviction within us that I am significant and important. The concept of God is humankind's attempt to explain the mysteries of life. God is at the centre of religion. Our image of God differs widely. We see Him as the one who created us and a world of so much beauty and goodness yet one who allows so much evil and absurdity. Different religions have vastly different interpretations.

Some focus on a god of power and glory, others on a god of wrath and vengeance. We recall the prophet Elijah in his famous confrontation with the prophets of Baal on Mount Carmel, how he mocked them, telling them to shout louder as Baal might be asleep and had to be awakened.

As Christians we believe in the God that Jesus revealed to us. He is the same God who spoke to the people on Sinai, who led the Jews through the Red Sea from the slavery of Egypt to freedom. He was sometimes seen as a jealous and passionate God who chastised the people when they sought after other gods, but was always faithful to the covenant He had made with His people. Later on it was seen that God was not only in love with his people but also with each individual person. Even though people might sin and do evil deeds, God was always ready to forgive and restore the friendship. Jesus revealed a God of goodness and compassion who loves us with an infinite love and wants us to love Him in return. Jesus is God's fingerprints on our human flesh and we need to immerse ourselves in the gospels to have some idea of the nature of God. The four gospels are magnificent portraits of Jesus and His mission.

In the Gospels Jesus has given us some insight into the mystery of God. So **we know that life has a meaning and our lives have a goal. We have a Father who cares for us, we have a Brother who died for us and we have a Spirit, a Comforter, who will guide us to the shores of eternity.**

Chapter Three

The Bible

For years the study of the Bible was neglected in Catholic teaching. Some considered it a Protestant book. In recent times we are encouraged to study the Bible. After all it is salvation history. It answers such questions as: who are we? What is the meaning of life? Is there a God who controls everything? Why is there evil in the world and what can we do about it? Is there an after-life?

We believe that the Bible is the word of God but to understand any passage we have to know something of the author, the cultural background, the people for whom he was writing, the purpose of his message and the language form he used... Is all scripture true? The Church states that *"the books of Scripture, firmly, faithfully and without error, teach that truth which God, for the sake of our salvation, wished to be confided to the Sacred Scriptures."*

The Bible is a religious book teaching us religious truths. The first chapters of Genesis are not to be taken literally. They are religious myths, beautiful stories containing religious truths, namely that God is the creator of all things, that all things are good, that man and woman are the high-point of God's creation, being created in His image and likeness, that the relationship between man and woman is essentially good and holy and that evil entered into our world by man's deliberate disobedience. The telling of the origin of evil has a certain psychological humour. When God challenged Adam he blamed Eve; when He challenged Eve she blamed the serpent and, as I tell the story, the serpent hadn't a leg to stand on! People are always looking for excuses for their evil deeds. Sometimes in confession when I asked a penitent why he did such a bad thing, the answer often was: the devil tempted me!

The Bible is not just one book but a whole library of books, seventy three in all, some historical, some prophetic, some of wisdom. It is divided into two major sections, the Old Testament and the New Testament. Here is another perspective:

I. The wonderful works which God performed through the Jewish people (O.T.)
II. The wonderful works which God performed through Jesus, His Son. (The four Gospels)
III. The wonderful works which God performed through the early Church. (The rest of the N.T.)

All was done in love for the sake of our salvation. The whole of S. Scripture is an invitation to accept our salvation and to play our part in bringing that salvation to others. Jesus is at the centre of the Bible. The whole of the Old Testament is a preparation for Jesus. The Gospels are stories or portraits of Jesus written for us, to make His whole life and teaching, His passion, death and resurrection in some way understandable. For the first Christians, the Resurrection was the wonderful event which gradually brought them to understand who Jesus really was. It gradually dawned on them that Jesus was the unique Son of God. The Resurrection was regarded as the moment when Jesus of Nazareth revealed Himself as the Son of God.

The Gospels were written with hindsight. Mark gives Jesus titles and describes events which point to His divinity. In both Matthew and Luke the understanding that Jesus is Lord and Saviour is reflected in the infancy narratives. The final step was one of pre-existence and this was revealed in John: *"In the beginning was the Word and the Word was with God and the Word was God."* John 1.

We live two thousand years later. As Christians we proclaim that Jesus is Lord. He is our Saviour, the unique Son of God who dwelt among us and redeemed us by His life, Passion, death and Resurrection. We are proud to follow Him and to live according to His teaching and thereby hope for Salvation.

Chapter Four

The four Gospels

The four Gospels are at the heart of the Bible. They are magnificent portraits of Jesus of Nazareth with special emphasis on His death and resurrection. They are both historical and religious books. They contain stories and events and the interpretation of these events, their meaning to those who experienced them.

The Gospels were written with hindsight, in the light of the Resurrection. They expressed the faith of the early Church, that Jesus of Nazareth who had suffered and died and had risen from death by the power of God and that He was truly the Son of God.

The ministry of Jesus began with a broad appeal to the public that the Kingdom of God was at hand. His healing miracles were signs of hope and salvation for all. His teaching was a radical challenge to all to rethink their religious ideas, their image of God, and the meaning of the law. Because the religious leaders of the day could not accept this, they saw Him as a threat to their leadership and so plotted His death. Jesus spoke with authority, was close to the poor and the marginalised and spoke of the dignity of each individual. He gave a message of great power and reconciliation.

The early Church saw that his passion and death were not the end but the beginning of new life, ushered in by the Resurrection. His disciples saw all that happened as the fulfilment of Sacred Scripture. The Resurrection was real but something outside the realm of earthly events. The Gospels treat it in different ways, referring mostly to the experience of the disciples.

I love the story of Pilate's wife. I think it's from John Masefield. She cannot sleep, knowing her husband had done a serious wrong. She comes to the tomb on Easter morn. She sees the stone rolled back and the centurion standing guard. *"Is he there?"* she asks. *"No, madam, he's not there." "Then, where is he?"* The centurion replies: *"Released to the whole world where neither Jew nor Roman can stop the power of His love."*

It was only after the Resurrection that the disciples began to understand the mystery of Jesus of Nazareth, the significance of his teaching, the meaning of His passion and death and the scandal of the Cross.

After the Resurrection the gathering of the disciples of Jesus under the leadership of Peter became the new People of God as distinct from the old groupings. In the light of the Resurrection they began to understand the teaching of Jesus, His life, His passion and death and they began to preach His message of salvation for all to the ends of the world. To help to achieve this, four Gospels were written on the teaching, the life, death and Resurrection of Jesus.

The gospels of Matthew, Mark and Luke are known as the Synoptics, because they follow the same pattern, the teaching and healing ministry of Jesus, ending with His death and

Resurrection and how Jesus of Nazareth was revealed as the Son of God. Theologians call this a low ascending Christology. John however begins his Gospel with the mystery of the Godhead: *"In the beginning was the Word, the Word was with God and the Word was God....The Word was made flesh and lived among us."* Theologians call this a high descending Christology.

The Gospels are unique testimony that Jesus of Nazareth was the Son of God. I'd like to add a few comments on two of them, namely that of Luke and that of John.

Chapter Five

The Gospel of St. Luke

This Gospel has been described as the loveliest book ever written. In it Luke sets out to write an ordered account of the life of Jesus. Luke is the one Gentile author in the New Testament. He was a doctor, a very cultured man and wrote in excellent Greek. His background would be vastly different from that of the Apostles. He was greatly influenced by St. Paul with a vision of Christ who came on earth to reconcile us all to God. His Gospel is a story of reconciliation. The parable of the prodigal son, told in chapter fifteen is in a way a summary of the whole gospel.

Jesus is the Redeemer, the Saviour of all people. This good news is meant for people of all times, everywhere. Luke's portrait of Christ is a very attractive portrait. One author writes that the Jesus of Luke might well have written the words on the statue of Liberty in New York harbour, *"Give me your tired, your poor, your huddled masses, yearning to be free. Send these, the homeless, the tempest-tossed to me."*

However in viewing the portrait of Christ there is a certain parallelism at work. The image of the gentle Christ is seen in the context of one whose time is short and whose demands on his followers are total. The cost of discipleship is real.

The structure of the gospel is clear. After the Infancy narrative we have the Galilean ministry. Then comes the travel narrative, the long journey to Jerusalem. This is unique to Luke, the contents of which are not matched in any of the other gospels. We have parables, controversies and miracles which tumble over one another in a magnificent panorama of the active Christ. He has advice and teaching for everyone and highlights the mistakes of those who would betray the nature of true religion.

Next comes the Jerusalem ministry ending with the account of the passion, death and resurrection of Jesus. For Luke, Jerusalem is the sacred place of destiny for Christ where He would redeem the world. In his follow-up book, the Acts of the Apostles, Luke describes how the good news of that redemption would be brought from Jerusalem to the ends of the world by the preaching of the Apostles and others.

Luke's gospel is a gospel of the poor. In the Infancy narrative it is the poor shepherds who were the first to be told of the birth of Jesus. Throughout his life, Jesus meets the poor, the lonely, the rejected, bringing the forgiveness and love of God to all of them. The Samaritans, the lepers, the widow of Naim, all have a special place in the concern and love of Christ. Luke also mentions a great number of women in his story that otherwise we would not have known about.

Luke mentions the presence and activity of the Holy Spirit and the importance of prayer. Throughout the gospel the theme is reconciliation. All people are called to be reconciled to God through Jesus Christ, our Saviour.

While the story of the prodigal son (or the prodigal father) in chapter fifteen of St. Luke's gospel, sums up beautifully the overall theme of Luke, there is another story which is worth recalling. It appears in St. John's Gospel but it is typically a story from St. Luke, originally dropped from the text as some thought Jesus was too soft on adultery and replaced in St. John's Gospel. No matter, it is the Word of God.

The woman taken in adultery. (John 8 3-11)

The weakest link is an interesting T.V. show. At the end of each round, one person (the weakest link) is ejected and sometimes humiliated by a rather stern presenter. The winner takes all. The rest get nothing. It's a good reflection on our age when we like to expose the mistakes and sins of others. That's why the tabloids are so popular. It can be a cruel world for some who are more sinned against that sinning. We are so quick to judge. There should be a better way. Jesus shows us that there is.

We look at John's Gospel, chapter eight. Let us imagine that scene outside the Temple in Jerusalem. A woman had been caught in the act of adultery and the scribes and Pharisees dragged her to the centre of the crowd. They thought they had a perfect case against the Master. Moses commanded that such a one should be stoned to death. What do you say? Jesus' reputation for love and forgiveness would now be put to the test. He could not deny the law of Moses.

We can see them waiting, some with hands bulging with stones ready to throw, the woman in the centre shaking with fear. We are told that Jesus bent down and started writing on the ground with his finger. It is the only mention in the Gospels of Jesus writing. What was he writing? Some say the sins of the accusers. Most likely he was playing for time, pondering on the injustice. If the woman was charged where was the man? When he did answer the challenge we can almost see his eyes blazing as He faced the crowd, *"If there is one among you who has not sinned, let him be the first to cast a stone at her."* We are told that they went away one by one, beginning with the eldest.

Jesus is left alone with the woman still trembling from the ordeal. But in the darkest moment of public exposure she hears the words of her Saviour, *"woman, has no one condemned you? ... Neither do I condemn you. Go and sin no more."* The Prodigal daughter arises with renewed energy to move out of the valley of darkness and reach for the heights of goodness. Yes there is a future as well as a past even for the weakest link.

The Acts of the Apostles

We cannot leave Luke without referring to his second book, The Acts of the Apostles. This is the story of the early Church combining history and theology. It deals mostly with Peter and Paul. The conversion of Paul on the road to Damascus had a profound effect on the early Church. Paul brought his vast knowledge of Sacred Scripture to show how the prophesies were fulfilled in Jesus. The Acts was written to strengthen the faith of the early Christians and to proclaim their right to practice their religion.

It tells how the salvation won for us by Jesus, the Good News of the Gospels, spread far and wide. Luke was a great friend of St. Paul and he describes in detail some of Paul's heroic journeys. Other than by a few learned people, the Gospel was spread mostly by ordinary women and men moved by the Spirit to give witness to the divinity of Christ. The Acts of the Apostles is sometimes called the Gospel of the Holy Spirit.

In the Acts the story is told through human lives. We get to know Peter and Philip, Barnabas and Paul and the difficulties they faced. We are caught up in the superstition, the idolatry and the black magic which permeated the pagan world then. The personal encounters between the missionaries and their opponents make for interesting reading. This interplay of personalities gives the book a remarkable vividness. We are plunged into the teaming life of the ancient Near East with its mixture of Jew and Gentile, the crowded streets and marketplaces, the mobs and the ghettos, the intellectuals and the magicians and confronting it all a handful of women and men afire with a new message of salvation and endowed with superhuman courage.

The first chapters deal with the growth of the early Christian community mostly around Peter. With the early persecution of the Christians the Gospel spreads to Samaria and Judea. Paul plays a dominant role in the final chapters. He is eventually arrested in Jerusalem. He appeals for his right to be taken to Rome to be tried. This is done and he continues to preach the Gospel even from his prison cell.

Rome is then the gateway to the whole world. The Good News must continue to be preached far and wide to the ends of the earth.

Chapter Six

Gospel of St. John

These things are written that you may believe that Jesus is the Christ, the Son of God, and that believing, you may have life in his name. (Jn. 20:21)

The eagle is the symbol of John's Gospel. It is claimed that the eagle is the only creature that can look at the sun without blinking. Certainly, with all its strength, it soars higher than any other bird to get closer to the sun. In the same way, many people find themselves closer to God and Jesus Christ by reading John's Gospel rather than any other book. It gives a profound insight into the significance of the person and work of Christ. The three synoptics begin with the nativity or public ministry of Jesus leading to His passion, death and Resurrection, revealing Jesus as the Son of God. We call this **a low ascending Christology.** John begins in the heart of the Godhead. *In the beginning was the Word... The Word became flesh and dwelt among us.* **(A high descending Christology).**

Certainly, St. John's Gospel is different. It contains many things that are not in the other Gospels, e.g. the raising of Lazarus from the dead. It does not mention the Institution of the Bl. Eucharist although Ch. 6 contains a beautiful passage on the Bl. Eucharist. Of the 29 miracles mentioned in the

Synoptics, John mentions only two and then adds five of his own. The 4 Gospels have things in common, of course. After all, they are portraits of the same person, Jesus of Nazareth.

Two main divisions in this Gospel are: **The book of signs (Ch. 1-12)** These chapters relate to **seven miracles** and seven great **I AMs.** The number seven for the Jews was the sign of perfection.

The second part of the Gospel (ch.13 to the end) **is called the Book of Glory.** The Last Supper is used by Jesus to give a long discourse on his teaching about the Father and about prayer. Ch. 17 is a magnificent chapter. Jesus consecrates his death as the way He would give glory to the Father and bring life to all of us.

The description of Calvary in John's Gospel is free of the terrible suffering and darkness of the other Gospels. It is the death of a man who proclaimed himself as the Lord of life, who lays down his life willingly, to the glory of the Father. The glory is already breaking through on Calvary as seen through the eyes of John.

In the Synoptics, the ministry of Jesus is centred in Galilee and Judea. In John His ministry is mainly in Jerusalem. The Synopics tell us of Jesus going up to the Holy City only once followed by the Last Supper and by His passion and death. (One year ministry) John refers to at least three visits. (Three year ministry)

The Gospel is attributed to John, the son of Zebedee and Salome. It was written sometime between 90 and 100 A.D., probably at Ephesus. John had time to reflect on his close friendship with Jesus and the Apostolic preaching after the Resurrection. His insights and experiences may have been written down by a disciple of John, as revealed to him by the Apostle, now an old man. John was the beloved disciple. He was the only one brave enough to stand on Calvary with the women. He was the one to whom Jesus entrusted His Blessed Mother before He died.

Chapter Seven

Who wants religion anyway?

"What you stand for, Reverend, is totally irrelevant in this day and age." The speaker didn't mean to be unkind. He was merely stating what for him and others was a fact of life. Religion might be alright for Ireland of the past or for primitive people of Africa or Asia, but in today's new world we can solve all our problems without taking God into account, thank you very much. Some ask what has religion done for people?

I think of an incident at Speakers Corner in Hyde Park, London, a well-known spot where anyone with a message to tell could stand on a soap box and shout away. It provided great entertainment to many people especially as hecklers were always interrupting the speakers. I enjoyed my few visits there.

One well known speaker was Fr. Vincent McNabb who gave powerful witness to Christian values in all his talks. Of course he was frequently heckled. On one occasion a rather nondescript, scruffy individual shouted up, *"Hey preacher, you talk of Christian values. How long is Christianity in the world and look at the state of affairs?"* Fr. McNabb ignored him for a while but when challenged that he had no answer, the priest looked at him and said, *"I will answer you, provided you answer my question first. Tell me how long is water in the world?"* The old hobo said, *"Millions of years, I suppose."* And Fr. McNabb said, *"And look at the state of your neck!"*

G.K. Chesterton once said, *"It's not a question of Christianity being tried and found wanting. It's a question of Christianity being difficult and not tried..."* Professing Christianity is one thing but it becomes a pretence unless we live according to the teaching of Christ. We should be known as Christians by our overall behaviour. As the little ditty puts it:

You are writing a gospel, a chapter a day
by the deeds that you do and the words that you say.
Men read what you write, if it's false or if it's true.
Now what is the gospel according to you?

The reality for the priest today is not irrelevance but rather that his message is very relevant as it is concerned with the great questions that face mankind, such as the meaning of life, social justice, the evil of so much violence, the poverty of some countries in a world of plenty. The teaching of Jesus Christ and His message of love and redemption and the dignity of each human person is very relevant as we face the great issues of today.

Life is often a bit of a mystery. We who believe in a personal loving God often ask why does God allow certain evil things to happen to good people. Why did He allow a young mother of three young children to die from cancer? Why does an all-powerful God allow accidents of nature to happen, such as a tsunami that destroys countless men, women and children? Why doesn't God answer my prayers? What did I do to deserve this? There are no easy answers to these questions.

The believing Christian must look to the person of Jesus. He did not run away from pain and suffering. He accepted the mockery, the scourging, the unjust trial, the death on the Cross and offered all up for our redemption. In the mystery of the Resurrection of Jesus, we can see suffering in a new light. It is part and parcel of the human condition and the example of Jesus gives us the inspiration to accept it and offer it up in union with Jesus for the redemption of the world.

Chapter Eight

The god I don't believe in

There was a book published some time ago called *"The god I don't believe in."* The author is Julian Arias and he makes some telling points. Certain religious practises and statements often hide the face of God and give a distorted image of the true God. I don't believe in a god who captures one by surprise in a sin of weakness and wants to condemn him. I don't believe in a god who condemns pleasure and material things, a god of fear and judgement, a god who is the monopoly of any one church, a magician god, a grandfather god. The only true image of God is that shown in the Bible. This image is vividly portrayed in the life and death of Jesus, whose perfect humanity was a unique disclosure of the mind and heart of God.

The concept of God remains a profound mystery which theologians and various scholars have wrestled with down the years. Isaac Newton was one of the greatest mathematicians and scientists that ever lived. He was also a deeply religious man and wrote on religion. He was acclaimed for his great achievements, the great truths he established which provided the foundation for others to build on.

Yet towards the end of his life he said of his achievements:

"I do not know what I appear to the world, but to myself, I appear to have been like a little boy playing on the seashore and diverting myself in now and then finding a smoother pebble, or a prettier shell than ordinary, whilst the great ocean of truth lay all undiscovered before me."

God remains a profound mystery. We can only turn to Jesus as the visible face of the invisible God. We read in St. Paul who wrote in his epistle to the Philippians, *"God has highly exalted him and bestowed on him the name which is above every name, that at the name of Jesus every knee should bow, in heaven, on earth and under the earth, and every tongue confess that Jesus Christ is Lord, to the glory of God the Father." (Phil.2 6-11)*

Today we are living in what is called **the post-modern world**. It is characterised by moral relativism (no absolute moral values) and individualism. There is a strong reaction against any big institution telling us what to do (the Church included), no objective truth or objective moral values. A lot depends on how I feel and the circumstances of the present moment. But in spite of much material progress there is also the sense of emptiness and futility among people today. The suicide rate in Ireland is appalling. So there is a search for spiritual values. Instinctively we know that man does not live on bread alone. The Mind, Body, Spirit section of our libraries and bookshops are well stocked. The Church needs to address this area. I suggest that the main elements of our Celtic Christian spirituality, as outlined in another chapter, have a lot to offer our people of today. Our religion is centred on the Bible and on the beautiful teaching of Jesus

Christ Our Saviour. It appreciates and cherishes nature, the body, women and community and sees God as spiritually present in our world and in all our activities.

Chapter Nine

Points to Ponder

1. I am a unique and precious human being, redeemed and loved by God.
2. I inherited a lot of gifts, talents and emotions, some positive, some negative; know thyself.
3. The sort of person I become depends on my use of intellect and free will. Develop the positive; control the negative.
4. I make decisions and take responsibility for them.
5. Often I'm not responsible for what happens to me; I am responsible for how I react to what happens to me.
6. Feelings are neither right nor wrong; what makes them moral is the way I handle them.
7. Bitterness, unforgiving attitudes, resentments, etc. are prisons which entrap me. The key to that prison is on the inside. Pray for the grace to forgive and be free.
8. Love your neighbour as yourself. Love yourself.
9. I live each day at a time. The journey of a thousand miles begins with one small step.
10. Personal reflection on experiences is a must for growth in maturity. Know thyself.

11. Yesterday is history; tomorrow is mystery; today is the only day we have; the present, a present from God. Live it to the full.

12. St. Paul to Ph. 4: 4, *"whatever is lovely, whatever is gracious, whatever is worthy of praise, fill your mind with these things and the God of Peace will be with you."*

Chapter Ten

The art of Preaching

In my life as a priest, I gave many retreats to young men preparing for Ordination. Twice in St. Patrick's College, Maynooth, in 1977 and in 1980, I gave the 6 day retreat to over sixty men who would be ordained in their own parishes within a week or two. It was a privilege and a challenge. I never preached down at them but rather shared my own efforts to live my priestly life to the full. A touch of humour is often very helpful.

The hen and the pig

In one Seminary where there were only a few for ordination, I felt there were a lot of distractions and to get their attention I told them a little story from my own background. I grew up on a small farm in the forties when the Great War was raging in Europe. I would catch a rabbit now and then and if we didn't have it for lunch, I sold it to a local man who exported some to England where food was very scarce. Some local authorities in Britain ran a campaign to encourage people to help with the situation. If you had a garden you could keep a few chickens and with a bigger garden, perhaps a pig or two. An attractive coloured poster was produced and was displayed in shop windows. It showed a typical English breakfast of rashers and eggs, with a catchy headline: *Help Britain win the war, produce more food.*

The story goes that Mr. Pig and Mrs. Hen were walking down Main Street when they spotted the poster. The hen stopped to cackle proudly and said to the pig: *"Mr Pig, oughtn't we be very proud of the part we are playing in helping Britain win the war."* The pig looked at the poster more glumly and said to the hen: *"Don't ever forget, Mrs Hen, that whereas yours is a mere contribution, mine is total commitment."* My ending to the students: *"don't forget young men, if you want to be a priest, it has to be total commitment".*

The art of preaching

For years in the Catholic Church the art of preaching was neglected. The priest saw his role as saying Mass and administering the sacraments. The only sermons I remember from boyhood were when the Redemptorists came round every few years to preach the parish mission. Then I heard all about the wrath of God, sin and damnation and the evil of sexual sins. Such sermons did little to enhance the two qualities needed for a genuine spiritual life, namely a healthy God image and a healthy self image. I quote from Fr. Vincent McNamara's book, **"The call to be human."**

"However it happened, the image that was handed down was of a God prying into every nook and cranny of life and of a church flushing sin from the coverts of our souls. How did we get from the Spring Flower of the New Testament to the sick worry of the confessional?"

After the second Vatican Council there was a great effort to encourage priests to improve their preaching. The Irish Hierarchy set up a Communications Centre in Dublin and encouraged priests to attend to improve their preaching skills. One story is told of a Bishop who called in one of his priests and told him: "*Now Fr. Paul, you are a very learned man in theology and Canon Law. But I'm afraid when you preach all that learning goes over the heads of your parishioners, as you are too intellectual and abstract. Now I'm going to sponsor you to attend a course in Dublin to enable you to communicate more effectively, in a language people can understand.*"

Fr. Paul didn't like the idea so he said to the bishop, "*My Lord, I'm too old for courses. You are far smarter than those people up in Dublin. You give me a few hints and that will do.*"

The bishop, not averse to a little flattery, said. "*Maybe you're right. I've been reading up on all this. There are two cardinal rules. Firstly, in this day of mass communication and multiple channels, you have to grab your audience in the first five seconds or they'll switch you off. Secondly, when you have their attention, speak in ordinary language, not in abstract ideas. For instance, we will soon have Holy Family Sunday. Don't talk about the past but tell them about your own father and mother, the values they had, the ideals they gave you.*"

Fr. Paul got very excited as he had so many happy memories of his parents. He could hardly wait for Holy Family Sunday. However, before he left he said to the bishop, "*I still have a problem. How do I grab the congregation in the first five seconds?*" The bishop smiled and said, "*I'll give you an opening that will grab their attention. You say slowly: the happiest moments of my life were spent in the arms of another man's wife. After a pause for effect you add: "she was of course my mother!"*

Fr. Paul was excited and could hardly wait for Sunday. But he was a bit forgetful and was afraid he'd lose his lines. He was nervous going to the pulpit so he began his sermon thus: *"My dear brethren, this is Holy Family Sunday, ah yes, a time to stress good relationships. I was in with the bishop during the week and do you know what he told me? He said that the happiest moments of his life were spent in the arms of another man's wife."* Fr. Paul then got confused, paused a long time and then blurted out, *"Gosh, I'm sorry, I forget who she was.!"*

Quick intelligent answers

Communication problems and the roving microphone affected many people in those days, especially business people who were expected to give a quick intelligent response when interviewed on T.V. or radio about their interests. One social club organised a Friday evening game to facilitate the speaking ability of the members. They had two boxes. One contained the names of the members. The other contained a wide list of topics, such as sport, politics, business, crime, immigrants, etc. A name was drawn from one box and from the other the subject he had to speak on for five to ten minutes. Members would give their verdict afterwards. It often provided good entertainment for the members.

One evening Jack's name was drawn and he waited nervously for the topic. It was sex. He felt a bit embarrassed but then realised his wife was not present, being at home with a cold. So he felt free to share a few jokes. When he got home that evening, his wife asked him about the speaker and the topic. He told her that he was the one, and then to avoid awkward questions he told her the subject was sailing. That was fine till a few days later his wife met a fellow member at the supermarket who told her: *"Your husband was terrific at his talk last Friday. He had us all in stitches."* The wife was rather puzzled and remarked, *"I can't see how he could be so good. We only did it twice and the second time his hat blew off."*

Good Advice

I return to the subject of preaching and the advice I give to the students preparing for the priesthood. I like the quote from Cardinal Martini: *"The Mass is offered by a community of faith and love and that community is formed and shaped by preaching the Word of God again and again."* In a good homily, the priest takes the word of God, breaks it and makes it digestible and nourishing for his people, just as later in the Mass, he breaks the sacred Host before distributing Holy Communion to nourish his people. One must make the Word of God relevant to the lives people live and their problems, hopes and fears. Karl Barth advised that one should preach with the Bible in one hand and the daily newspaper in the other.

A homily should be challenging and it often has to address itself to the evils of the times we live in. But it should be more full of encouragement then condemnation. It should always reflect the good news of the Gospel in which we celebrate the victory of Christ over sin and death. The good news of the Gospel is that God loved us so much that he gave His only Son to die on the cross for our salvation and that those who believe in Him may have eternal life.

Rivalry

In religious congregations who used to give parish missions there was often rivalry between members as to who was the best preacher. I had heard that a certain priest had a good reputation and asked a fellow member about him. He was obviously not impressed and said, *"Well, he preaches long enough anyway. His sermons are like big steer, a point here, a point there and a lot of bull in between!"*

One preacher anxious to gain a little confidence asked one of the congregation if he enjoyed his sermon and which passage he liked best, the parishioner said, *"Your passage from the pulpit back to the altar."*

I was once preaching a retreat to a sizable group of marriage couples and to lighten the mood at the end I told them this story.

God once sent his archangel Michael to do a survey on all the married couples in this county and how they had behaved, if they had kept their marriage promises fully. He found that there were only five couples who were completely faithful. God told the archangel to write a letter of commendation and to give them a special blessing and further instructions on their relationships. Now the punch line question: what did the angel write?

In answer to a long silence, my question is: *"What, did none of you get the letter?"*

Someone said a good sermon should be like a mini-skirt, long enough to cover the subject, short enough to be interesting. You stand up to be seen, speak up to be heard and shut up to be appreciated.

Chapter Eleven

Stories from my pastoral ministry

What does a Bishop read?

Sharing one's belief in Christ and His message of salvation with different groups of people is a great privilege. In my time I have addressed various groups, including army personnel, business people, priests and bishops. I was once asked to give some talks to the army men stationed in Longford. The first morning some officers invited me in to share morning coffee with them. I thanked them but told them that Bishop Cahal Daley who was then the local bishop had already invited me to his house. I had given the priests retreat in Longford the year before and he knew me well. Said one of the officers: *"you might ask him what literature is he reading nowadays."* Knowing bishop as a very well read man, I was curious about the question but the officer would not explain further.

I had a pleasant session with the bishop chatting about various current affairs. Before I left I asked the question the officer had posed. The bishop shook his head and blurted out *"Oh, that occasion."* That made me more curious so I told him he had better explain. The story went like this.

The bishop had been on a radio discussion panel and the subject was feminism. He felt he did O.K. but there were books mentioned which he hadn't read. He made a note of them and when he got home he asked his secretary to order them from Veritas. The next day the secretary told him that three of those books were banned in the Republic. After a while the bishop pointed to a solution. He said, *"I used to lecture in Queen's University in Belfast and I still have an account there. Ask them to send the books under plain wrapper and charge them to my account."*

A few days later a Garda came to see the bishop and to warn him that the I.R.A. were sending out some parcel bombs and as he had so often condemned the I.R.A. violence, he might be a likely target, so he should be careful. Two days later a parcel arrived for him under plain wrapper. Forgetting his order from Belfast he became alarmed and called the police. The police called the army who arrived with a type of tractor with a long robot arm which grabbed the parcel and took it down to the barracks square. They blew the end off and out hops four books with rather interesting titles such as The Female Eunuch by Germaine Greer. So that is what the Bishop reads!! It became a source of great laughter.

A trip in the air

I enjoyed my stay with the army. I was free in the afternoon and one of the trainee pilots took me up for a spin in a small chipmunk. He was there to practice his aviation skills. There was room only for the two of us. We had to wear parachutes in case of trouble. I guessed the commander had told the pilot to give the chaplain a few frights when airborne. The pilot flew high, did a few stunts, flew upside down and sideways. Then he asked me if I was O.K. In fact I enjoy flying and this was a great experience. Under the pilot's instructions, I took over the controls and with a steady hand I could guide the plane. For a while I was like a child playing with a huge toy in the air.

When Ireland had capital punishment

As National Director for Vocations, I had many contacts with the bishops of Ireland. Bishop Joseph Carroll told me that he had once been a prison chaplain and was the last priest in Ireland to be present at public executions. He told me he assisted on six occasions, six men of different ages and backgrounds, all condemned for murder. They had all made their peace with God and attended Mass which Fr. Carroll offered in their cell next to the point of execution. He told me one interesting thing. Without exception, they were all very scared and shaking. But once he gave them Holy Communion a great peace came over them. They seemed to get the courage to face the awful moment of truth. They all refused the proffered glass of whiskey and walked bravely onto the scaffold. A man called Pierepoint was brought over from England as the executioner. He once had to shout at Fr. Carroll who was standing too near the trap-door. He fixed the noose on the prisoner and it was all over in a matter of seconds. Thank God capital punishment was abolished in Ireland soon afterwards.

Clerical dress

In this day and age when anything goes it's hard to realise how the bishops insisted that all priests should wear black clerical dress in public and always wear a hat. Archbishop John Charles McQuade of Dublin was known to publicly correct priests who were not properly attired. He was known to stop his car, call the priest over and rebuke him. However on one occasion when he saw a cleric the other side of the street, he sent his secretary over with the message, *"His Grace, the Archbishop of Dublin, demands that you wear a hat when walking in public."* The answer was more than he had bargained for. *"Tell the Archbishop to mind his own business and as an Archbishop myself I will wear whatever I want."*

A certain priest in Dublin who was a good mimic and with a great sense of humour developed the practice of imitating the various accents of country people. When he realised he could imitate the voice and accent of Dr. McQuade to perfection, he used it to play tricks on some of his colleagues, ringing them up, pretending he was the archbishop and speaking of all sorts of rumours and a possible transfer. He got a lot of fun out of that. However, one victim who was fooled once too often, got a call one evening from the real Archbishop. When he heard him say, *"This is his Grace speaking…,"* he cut in sharply and told His Grace in no uncertain manner to F…off.

McQuaid to his credit took it in good fun when he heard the reason.

A midnight drama

Strange things do happen. A few years back I was driving my car late one night on my way to Navan, where I was staying with my sister, Teresa. Somewhere outside Delvin as I rounded a bend on the road which had a wide grassy margin, I saw a strange sight. A car was at the side of the road and standing in the grass were two priests that I knew. Each had a girl clinging to him. You could not have imagined the scene. As I jumped out to enquire what in heaven's name was happening, another girl rushed towards me. She shouted at me, *"Help me. They're coming back."*

Down the road, I saw a big van which was slowing down and stopping. The two priests were glad of my presence and I asked for some explanation for this extraordinary scene. Apparently the girls were at a dance and accepted a lift home from two men in a van. At this point on the road the men stopped the van and tried to molest the girls who struggled and screamed and managed to jump out of the vehicle. When they saw a car coming the van drove off. Two priests got out of the car and the girls rushed to them and sought help. Then I arrived and the third girl rushed over to me. What a scene!

Anxious to do something, I disentangled myself from a clasping female and walked down to the parked van. Two men glared at me from inside. I deliberately took out a pen and notebook and took down the number. *"What are you doing here?"* I asked. *"We can park anywhere we like,"* one of them said. I replied, *"Fine, just stay here till the guards arrive, because I'm going to call them and tell them how you molested those girls." "We never touched them,"* said one, as they drove away.

I went back to the girls and the two priests and arranged to take them home as they lived not too far away. We first went to the police in Delvin and reported the matter.

As one of the girls recognised the two men, I believed they were later charged. I don't know the result as I went abroad shortly afterwards. I only have a memory of three priests with three frightened females on a lonely dark road after midnight. You couldn't have invented such a scene.

Pennies from Heaven

There is a beautiful shrine in upstate New York in honour of three Jesuit martyrs who died when preaching the Faith to the Mohawks in the 17th century. The priests were martyred in 1647. The shrine is in Auriesville about 40 miles from Albany. I was working in the area and visited the shrine on many occasions and found it a wonderful place for reflection and prayer. Many pilgrims came to pray there and some left written petitions. Once when I visited there a local gentleman told me an interesting story of one such petition.

Mrs Brown (not her real name) lived in the area. She was not exactly gospel-greedy but did pray occasionally at the shrine. She was now in dire straits and needed money badly. She had a mortgage to pay, kids to feed, and a few debts piling up. Someone suggested that she pray for help and what better place than at the shrine? She went there and said a few scattered prayers. Out of curiosity she looked at some of the petitions and a few flowers and pictures near one statue. She picked up one bulky envelope and gave a cry of delight at seeing what it contained, a large bundle of dollars. This surely was an answer to her prayer. She slipped quietly away with her treasure and told no one

Meanwhile back at the Monsignor's house the phone rang. A voice called. *"Are you the man in charge of the shrine?"* *"Yes, what can I do for you?"* The gentleman on the phone said, *"I received a great favour when I did a novena of prayer to the Jesuit martyrs. My son recovered from a serious illness. I wish to remain anonymous but, in thanksgiving, I left a donation of a thousand dollars at the shrine. It would be wise to collect it immediately. It's in a brown paper bag. No, I do not wish to give my name."*

The Monsignor went to check but at the door met a friend who delayed him a bit. On going to the shrine and searching, he found nothing, and he had no way to contact the person who made the phone call.

Roll on the years. The woman in question was again in need of cash. This time she confided to friends how she had prayed at the Shrine five years before and how quickly (as she put it) God had answered her prayer. The word got around. The Monsignor heard the story, checked the date and knew what had happened to the anonymous donation. There was little he could do about it; the money was gone and that was that.

Chapter Twelve

Officiating at weddings

It has been my privilege to officiate at many weddings down the years, in different countries and in different cultural backgrounds. It can be quite exciting in Africa when the pastor lines up forty or fifty couples together to have their unions blessed in the sacrament of marriage. They have been living together in what they consider a genuine marriage but are reluctant to have a church wedding as too expensive. So the common celebration, funded by the parish, solves that problem.

A wedding is one of life's great occasions, a time to sing songs and dream dreams, to hold the hand of the person most dear to you, to say the most important words two people can say to each other and together to face whatever the future holds. Whenever I officiate I try to make it a real celebration of joy.

When it comes to the exchange of vows I remind the couple that they confer the sacrament upon each other as they make their vows. Vows strengthen our natural weaknesses. They confirm us in our desire to do good. They bring out the best in us. So my one bit of counselling to the couple after they have exchanged their vows is a quote from a famous German Lutheran pastor, Dietrich Bonhoeffer, who was executed for his opposition to Hitler. On one occasion when he was officiating at a wedding he addressed the couple in these words; *"Today you are very much in love and you think your love will sustain your marriage. It may not, but let your marriage vows always sustain your love for each other."*

Priests are usually invited to the reception afterwards and also to say a few words. In my own case many of the guests have heard me before so one must try to vary the theme and find some original jokes. This is often difficult. But here are a few samples.

A manufacturer of computers in France had a successful export business. In the instruction booklet in English the computer can be listed as it, but in French is has to be referred to by its gender, so the question is: should it be he or she. The workforce was divided into two groups, men on one side, women on the other, to discuss the matter. The women were unanimous. Computers must be listed as male. Reasons:

- You have to switch them on to get any good out of them.
- They are supposed to solve the problem but mostly they are the problem.
- They are full of details but often clueless.
- When you commit yourself to one model, you find afterwards that you could have got a much better model for the same price.

The men however decided that computers were feminine to the core:

- Their internal functions are known only to their creator.
- The language they use to communicate to each other is unintelligible to any outsider.
- Your smallest mistake is stored away in their long term memory, to be recalled again at a most inconvenient time.
- When you commit yourself to one model, you'll find yourself spending half your salary buying accessories for it.

Your verdict...?

Getting tipsy

At weddings there is often a long delay between the reception and the meal. There is plenty of time to have a few drinks. Many want to treat the priest, so one has to be careful. *"No thanks, not another drink, I don't want to get tipsy as I have to drive home."* I'm fortunate in that I don't have any great problem with drink. *"But Father, did you never get tipsy?"* My festive friends pressed me hard. They wanted a story, so why not give them one?

I was at a big wedding over in the United States and there was far too much drinking and perhaps I had taken too much. But I felt all right and when I decided to go home, I looked for my car keys. They were in my jacket on the back of a chair. A gentleman helped to find them but rather than hand them over he told me sharply, *"Father, you're in no condition to drive. I'll look after your car. You take a bus or a taxi."* I protested that I was O.K. but with no success. I had about twelve miles to go to where I was staying. The hotel was part of a huge trading centre with plenty of buses and taxis outside. Some of my friends were quite amused as I pretended to stumble on the way out.

I took a bus and away I went. On the road there were two police checks. They were stopping every car but waved the bus through. So when I got home I was very relieved. Reason: I had never driven a bus before.

What do you call the baby?

I have another story from Africa which I like to tell when someone indicates that we priests have little experience of the challenges of life. I make the boast that I have probably taken more pregnant women to hospital than any married man at the reception. In Africa babies are usually born at home. People only call for help when the woman is suffering and in danger.

One night well after midnight I was called. A pregnant woman was in trouble and could I take her to the mission hospital where there was a doctor in residence. In haste I put an old mattress and a couple of blankets on the back of my Toyata pick-up. Two women helped the suffering mother and knelt by her and off we went. The hospital was ten miles away. I drove fast but had to be careful on a bad road. Suddenly there was a cry of alarm. She was about to give birth. We were near a compound where people lived. I blew the horn to attract attention and two other women arrived to help. There was a happy ending as a baby boy was safely delivered. I continued to the hospital and called the doctor who complemented the helpers. I felt so relieved and delighted that all was well.

There is a custom in Africa to call the baby after someone or in memory of some important event, such as a storm or an accident… I helped on many occasions so there are one or two Christophers around. This particular family later sent a message of thanks to me and said the baby was called after me. I thought of possibilities, Christopher, Fr. Chris, or perhaps Fr. Fox. When I asked what the baby's name was they said, we called him Toyota!!

Chapter Thirteen

A touch of humour.

"Blessed are those who can laugh at themselves,
they will have no end of fun."

Golf should be fun

Priests seek relaxation in many different ways. I found the weekly game of golf very enjoyable. When I was in Courtfield I joined a club in Cardiff which offered reduced membership fees to clergymen. Every Monday over twenty priests would meet, divide up in fours for a local competition. We would meet for a meal afterwards. It was a very pleasant diversion from the daily work load.

Golfers of course never cheat although one of our members was not averse to kicking his ball out of the rough if there was nobody looking. Nobody minded. It was all good fun. However once when he won a minor prize I told this story at the presentation.

Smith and Jones were deadly rivals in a local club. They had the same handicap but each claimed he could beat the other. The only way to settle the matter was a straight eighteen holes head-to-head battle on a certain date. The contest began. They matched each other, hole after hole, one down, one up, equal, till they reached the last hole, the 18th, all square. Jones hit a magnificent drive down the middle within easy reach of the green. Smith hit a long shot too but the ball curled into thick rough at the end. Jones hit his ball onto the green and then went to help Smith look for his ball. Officially one is allowed five minutes to find a lost ball, so impatiently Jones soon cried out that the time was up. But Smith claimed there was still some time left. Then he shouted that he had found his lost ball and sure enough, he pointed to a ball sitting up on level piece of ground within easy reach of the green. Now the question is this: What would you do if you were Jones who had actually found the lost ball and had it safely in his pocket?

Is there golf in Heaven?

Two priests who were close friends used to play golf every Monday down the years. As old age was catching up on them a discussion arose as to the possibility of playing golf in heaven. So they made a pact: whoever would die first would come back and inform his friend.

In God's good time, one of them died. His friend got a mighty shock that night, awaking from a slumber, to find the ghost of his golf partner standing by the bed. When he got over the shock and the ghost reminded him of the promise, he cheered up and asked for the answer, yes or no. When the ghost hesitated, it made him wonder. After all, there was only one question. Is there golf in heaven? The ghost assured him *"yes, there were many magnificent courses there."*

His friend then asked why the hesitation, why the delay and the ghost said slowly, *"You see, I looked at the notice board before I came to see you and I saw that you are due to play there on Saturday week."*

Lee Trevino became a champion golfer from once being a lowly caddie. He never lost his sense of humour, chatted freely when playing and once pulled a snake out of his bag in a non-important match. He bought a sizeable property for his wife and family. Some evenings he loved to don work clothes and do the gardening. He tells of one incident when he was mowing the lawn. A lady in a posh Cadillac pulled over her car and shouted across to him, *"Boy, come here; do you speak English?" "Yes ma'am,"* he replied. *"What do you charge for work like that?"* Lee tells it with a straight face as he said, *"The lady of the house lets me sleep with her!"* You could hardly see the Cadillac for the dust as the caller sped away

If you are talking about the sport when ladies are present, avoid discussing the origin of the word GOLF. The canny Scots who claim they invented the game and looked for a good name tell us it means **G**entlemen **O**nly, **L**adies **F**orbidden.

It must be admitted that some take their golf too seriously. One golfer arrives back at the clubhouse carrying a dead body. He goes up to the bar, orders a double whiskey and sighs. *"Poor old Brown"* he said, *"collapsed at the 12th and died."* A customer said, *"It must have been a terrible job carrying him back all that way." "Yes, but the really tiring thing about it was having to put him down and pick him up again every time I had to play a shot."*

Was it the same man who during a tense golf match suddenly paused, took off his cap, bowed his head as he pointed to the highway. His companions could see a funeral procession slowly passing by. One of them complimented him on his great respect for the dead. His reply was that that was the least he could do after forty years of marriage.!!

Let us consider other sports

As I happen to think that our Irish game of hurling is the best game in the world, I put in this prayer as a tribute to the many outstanding players I have seen over the years.

A hurler's prayer

Grant me, O Lord, a hurler's skill
With strength of arm and speed of limb,
Unerring eye for the flying ball
And courage to match them what e're befall.
May my aim be steady, my stroke be true.
My actions manly, my misses few;
And no matter what way the game may go
May I part in friendship with every foe.
When the final whistle for me is blown,
And I stand at last at God's judgement throne
May the great Referee when He calls my name
Say "You hurled like a man,
You played the game."

When you compare the excitement and passion of a good game of hurling with the monotony of cricket, you see the contrast. George Bernard Shaw once said, *"The English, not being a very religious nation, God gave them cricket to give them some idea of eternity."* If you need some explanation of how cricket is played let me tell you. When you read this all should be very clear!

You have two sides, one out in the field and one in.
Each man that's in the side that's in goes out
And when he's out, he comes in
And the next man goes in until he's out.
And when they are all out, the side that's out comes in
And the side that's been in goes out
And tries to get those coming in out.
Sometimes you get men still in and not out.
When both sides have been in and out
Including the not-outs,
That's the end of the game. HOWZATT111

The executive jet

At a time when I was based in England in certain circles Irish jokes became popular. These were harmless enough meant to highlight the dim-wittedness or mental slowness of certain people. However once as an appropriate response I told my own version. It went like this.

I once managed to get a lift out of Heathrow on a special executive jet which carried three very important people on special assignments. Firstly, there was Miss U.K. going to take part in the Miss Universe competition. Then there was the Brain of Britain due to compete in the Brain of the World challenge. Thirdly there was the chief Boy Scout of Britain taking part in a World Jamboree. The space was cramped so they had to store all their luggage overhead with the parachutes.

Five minutes after take-off, the pilot came back to announce drastic news. He told them he had forgotten to refuel. There was only a few minutes flying time left. He had pointed the plane out to sea. They would be over land for about five minutes, so they had better be ready to jump. However there was a further problem which he pointed out as he opened the locker overhead and the parachutes came tumbling down with most of the luggage. There were only four parachutes for five on board so a hard decision had to be made. Obviously as pilot he would have to report on all this, so he grabbed a parachute and jumped. Whereupon, Miss U.K. said it would be unthinkable for the one lady not to be next, so she took a parachute and jumped. Then the Brain of Britain declared that there was still no reason for a moment's delay. Just think of the loss he would be to Britain, compared with a boy scout or some old preacher, so just get out of my way. He grabbed, strapped on and jumped.

There were just the two of us left, so I told the boy scout that we priests were supposed to be ready for death at any time and that I was happy to let him have the last parachute. But be sure to tell the people what I did for him. The scout answered, *"Not at all, Father, we both strap on parachutes and we can jump together."*

I pointed out that there must be only one parachute left but the scout answered, *"There are two. You see that Brain of Britain strapped on my haversack instead of a parachute."*

Detective skill

Sherlock Holmes and Dr. Watson decided to go camping one summer evening to relax a little after some difficult work. They pitched camp in a grassy area among some trees. Their tent was of strong canvas to protect against any possible rain. They were soon sound asleep in their sleeping bags. However Holmes thought he had heard some noise in his sleep and gradually woke up and looked up. He reached over and poked Watson and called him to wake up. Watson opened his eyes and Holmes told him: *"Look up, Watson. What do you see?"* Watson said, *"I see an array of beautiful stars looking down on us." "What does it mean?"*said Holmes. Watson replied *"It means the Creator is sending His light to the distant galaxies." "For God's sake wake up"*, said Holmes. *"It means that our tent has been stolen."*

Dinny the spy

Only a few years ago, the Russians opened an embassy in Orwell Road, quite near us. In contrast to the other houses on this grand road it is well fortified with high wall and barbed wire. There were various rumours of spies and secret agents but the story I like best is this one.

Apparently they had a top agent working in Ireland for a long time. He had an assumed name of Dinny O'Shea and was based mostly down in Kerry. As he had not reported for some time the KBG sent an agent to locate him. The password was *"The brown cow is in the green field."* Travelling through the highways and byways of Kerry the agent went into a popular bar to listen to the local chatter. The barman seemed well informed on local events so the agent went up to him and asked, *"Would you know anyone around here by the name of Dinny O'Shea?"* Said the barman, *"Which Dinny? You see there's Nell's Dinny, Dinny the Post and Dinny that keeps greyhounds. And as a matter of fact, I'm Dinny O'Shea myself."* The agent thought carefully: a barman, hears a lot, cool customer, possibly the one, so he said carefully to him, *"Do you know that the brown cow is in the green field?"*

The barman laughed and said, *"Yerra man, why didn't you say that in the first place? You're looking for Dinny the spy. He lives over in the next village, near the forge."*

To end this chapter, let me give you a little piece on St. Christopher. The name means **"Bearer of Christ."**
"As long as you did it to one of these, the least of my brethren, you did it unto me."

St. Christopher who was beloved by the Lord
And lived all alone in a hut by the ford.
When travellers came by night or by day
He used to carry them over the way.

One night when the weather was wintry and wild
He heard his name called by the voice of a child.
O Christopher, Christopher,. Christopher, come,
O Christopher, Christopher, carry me home.

The saint was surprised when the crossing began,
To find him as heavy as any grown man,
But when he was over, he found to his joy
It was Christ he had carried as well a boy.

Chapter Fourteen

Uganda in the sixties

When I went to Uganda in 1961 the country was then a British Protectorate, not a colony. All the ex-pats were diplomats, teachers, government officials, workers in the various industries or traders. The tourism industry flourished then as Uganda had much to offer. The Queen Elizabeth or Murchison Falls game parks had an abundance of game, an incredible variety of wild life, including elephants, rhinos, giraffes, many kinds of antelopes, warthogs, hyenas and wild dogs. One could almost (metaphorically) walk across the river Nile on the backs of hippos and you could guide a boat close enough to the banks to study the many crocodiles basking in the sunshine. The country was very much at peace. One could travel up-country or spend some time in the capital, Kampala, without much danger. Our missionaries worked very hard to develop the country. The mission compound was a great centre of activity, reaching out to people in all their needs. Schools were established, and also health-care centres and mission hospitals.

My first sick-call

I was working in a big parish outside Soroti, a town in the north-east, learning the local language and enjoying the challenge of pastoral work dealing with problems far removed from an Irish situation such as polygamy and witchcraft. My first late night call was in response to a little girl who came screaming to my door, *"come quickly, daddy is killing mammy."* I knew enough of the language to get the message and rushed out and followed her along the path to her home. I charged in. Sure enough a man was beating hell out of his wife. She was screaming and bleeding badly. I grabbed the man by the throat, wrenched the stick out of his hand and pushed him against the wall. Yes, when you are six foot four and used to rugged Gaelic football, it gives you a certain advantage in these circumstances. He quickly submitted. The woman ran out. I took the man to the local police station and accused him of attempted murder. The local policeman just smiled. Wife-beating is certainly not attempted murder. Anyway, I warned the man not to beat his wife ever again. I would be watching him and I felt quite pleased with my small contribution to the well-being of one poor woman.

Hunting for hippo

Aloet College was a big secondary school in our parish and Fr. Louis Albers was chaplain there. He liked to do a bit of hunting at times and he possessed two powerful hunting rifles. Most game were protected and one required a license to shoot certain animals. Fr. Louis was anxious to shoot a hippo as there were many in Lake Kioga nearby. The local people could eat the meat. It would be a great boost to their meagre diet. He invited me to take part in the hunt. A local guide instructed us as follows. Hippos leave the water and come out to graze only after the sun goes down. Although they have thick skin, it is sensitive to sun rays. They spend a couple of hours grazing before returning to the water. Our plan was simple. You wait patiently in the tall shrubs or high grass near the lake. Certain movements will tell you if a hippo is within range. Be sure that you don't get between the animal and the water. We had powerful torches strapped to the barrels of the guns. The idea was to take careful aim at the beast, switch on the torch and blind him for a few seconds. That will give you time to shoot. Aim for the heart and hope for the best. That was the theory.

In fact we waited for over an hour in the darkness, about thirty yards apart. Nothing happened. We moved about a little with no sign of a hippo. We gave up and returned to our starting point. This was a big compound with about thirty men sitting around beer pots drinking the local brew called ajon. One drank it through straws which were passed around. Women kept the big pots topped up. There was laughter and story-telling. You were most welcome to join in the drinking. The local beer from millet can be quite strong and nourishing. I took a few sips but I didn't have a taste for it, so I looked for a place to sit, free from mosquitos. The best place was near a fire allowing the smoke to act as a deterrent. We had come a long way and the guide said we should wait till near morning when the hippos would emerge again and perhaps we would have better luck. The locals remarked that we didn't look like big game hunters and they were right. At about four a.m. we ventured forth again and took up stations. I walked around a little and waited. Then I thought

I heard an animal moving. I raised my rifle, finger on the torch trying to make out the exact location. Suddenly, without warning a huge hippo charged passed me and I heard him plunge into the lake. Thank God I was not in his way! We waited further but nothing happened. Then at dawn the guide had another idea. He had a boat nearby. We should row out a little. The hippos often rose a bit out of the water. We could have a good shot at one of them then. We did get into the boat and rowed out a little. Suddenly the situation struck me. A good snort from a hippo would be enough to capsize the boat and drown us all. I ordered an immediate return to the shore and that was the end of our first hunting safari.

My second hunting safari

This came a couple of years later. My colleague and close friend, Fr. Eddie Bennett, had two brothers working in Tanzania or as it was then called Tanganyka. Both were married and had professional jobs and were living in the vicinity of Arusha, a busy market town. We spent our vacation with them on a few occasions. They had land rovers and hunting equipment and it was so pleasant to visit the game parks around, teeming with wild life. Game was protected although some poaching went on. Elephants were often killed for the ivory. I was once offered a tidy sum to smuggle some items to Europe. You needed a licence to shoot some named animals. One of the most valuable trophies was the antlers of a giant kudu. They were magnificent to see, curling, twisting and often spreading out over ten feet apart. I hated to see any of those animals killed but Derek Bennett had permission to shoot one kudu and he asked his brother and myself to come along with him.

The land was covered with bushes and shrubs but there were some fairly well defined paths to guide us. On the evening of the first day our local guide had to be taken home and I was asked to do so. He lived with his wife and family about three miles away. It was evening and we reached his home without difficulty. It was now dark and my problem was to find my way back safely to where we were camped. I drove carefully and after about a mile I came to a fork in the road. I felt I should take the left fork but suddenly I noticed a stray dog on the other side. He was wagging his tail and almost beckoning me to follow him. I did so but soon lost sight of him. I felt like turning back but then I noticed a large hut on the right, in off the road.

I realised that I had not come this way. I had one of the hunting rifles in the land-rover and before I left I had arranged with my companions that if I did get lost I could fire a single shot in the air and wait sixty seconds for a reply. I stopped the vehicle, pointed the gun out the window and fired a single shot. I waited for the reply but then there was a sudden development.

From the big hut three men rushed out and raced to a compound a hundred yards away. They must have thought I was a robber. I heard a distant reply to my rifle shot and was about to turn the car when I heard a faint cry for help from the big hut. I pointed the headlights towards the hut, took my gun and walked gingerly to the opening. In the shadows I could see three youths, hands bound and tied to some fixture. It was some surprise. I got a large knife from the car and was able to cut them loose. It transpired that they were Uganda boys who had come to Tankanyka looking for work and were captured as slaves. They were overjoyed when I spoke a few words of their tribal language. I ushered them to the land-rover, fired a couple of shots to deter any possible followers and within an hour was safely back with my companions. Apparently at that time many Ugandan youths were lured into some sort of slave racket. They were trapped and I fortunately liberated three of them. Later I gave them their fares back to Uganda.

At the campsite at night we slept in our sleeping bags around a big fire. It could keep us warm if the night got chilly but more importantly it kept wild animals away. If someone woke up the instructions were to pile more wood on the fire.

I was glad when morning came. We had a bit of breakfast and then prepared to launch out on our safari for giant kudu. Derek had a permit to shoot one.

We toured the hills and valleys all morning with no success. Then as we were about to give up we mounted a gentle slope and lo and behold about a hundred and fifty yards away stood a giant kudu. Derek stopped the car, took his powerful rifle, adjusted the sights and took careful aim. The kudu looked magnificent, his huge antlers reflecting the sun as he trotted away unaware of the danger. Derek took careful aim and fired. I must confess that at that moment I prayed that he would miss. I couldn't bear to see that beautiful animal struck to the ground. The report of the gunshot echoed loudly over the whole valley. The kudu raised his head in alarm and galloped hastily away. Derek had missed. I expressed my regret but secretly I was delighted.

The game parks in East Africa were great attractions for tourists, enabling them to see a wide variety of wild life close up. There were of course strict rules to be obeyed. Always respect the welfare of the animals and don't go too close to them especially if their young are around. Keep the windows in your car closed if any approach your vehicle

Once I got too close to shrubs concealing a lioness and her cubs. Her roar was a salutary warning. On another occasion a rhino took exception to my presence and came charging. I was in a solid land-rover so as he thumped the steel frame of the car his horn came off worst. Giraffes are beautiful creatures. I remember when two of them came up to my car and just stood there so I examined their long necks at close quarters. The Ngorora crater in Tanzania, several miles wide must have the greatest and most varied forms of wildlife anywhere from elephants to warthogs, from wildebeest to hyenas. One could view all kinds of animals in their natural habitat.

Some animals can be tamed. A white farmer in north Kenya had a big lion who would wander around his farmyard in the day. The house-boy would lock him up at night. One night when the farmer was out at a party and had a bit too much to drink, he found a lion sleeping at his front door that gave a growl when disturbed. A good kick sent him down the steps. He called his servant and asked why he had not locked the lion. *"But I did,"* said the servant and pointed to the caged lion. The farmer was suddenly sober, realising his narrow escape.

Chapter Fifteen

Snakes alive

Snakes were very common in Uganda and were rightly feared as the poisonous ones caused a lot of deaths. Sometimes when driving, if I ran over a snake trying to cross the road, there was great applause from my passengers. I had a couple of lucky escapes myself. Once walking in the dark in a wooded area, I thought I saw a movement ahead. I stopped to look. There in front of me just yards away were two hooded cobras. They were raised up ready to strike. I gave them a wide berth.

On another occasion I was reading late at night in my small bed-sit and I felt it was time to roll in. Suddenly I sensed there was a slight movement in the room. I looked carefully and sure enough I saw a snake's tail protruding from under the bed. It looked like a black mamba which is deadly poisonous. Now what to do? I couldn't take my eyes off it lest he'd escape or hide somewhere else. Sitting at my narrow desk, I sought some weapon. The only thing I could find with my groping left hand was a heavy hard-covered book. It was the Jerusalem bible. Flushing the snake out by throwing another book, it bolted across the floor and I managed to chop its head with my heavy book. In telling the story later I said that I killed it with the Axe of the Apostles!

Snakes can surface in the most unlikely places. One poor lady while relieving herself in a primitive loo was bitten by a snake that rose from the bottom. Fortunately she was able to get help but the incident didn't exactly help her digestion!

Safari ants were common in Uganda. Literally tens of thousands of them move along in a narrow column. Just avoid them when walking, easy in daytime but often in the dark if you make the mistake on treading on them you pay the consequences when thousands creep up your legs.

I once had a strange encounter with them. Before I went to bed I made sure the mosquito net was safely in place with no holes in it as I felt they were the only danger. I was sound asleep when around midnight I was suddenly awakened with ants crawling all over me. They had found their way through the makeshift door, climbed onto the bed and had a big body to feed on. I sprang up ripping my pyjamas off. Fortunately I had a toilet and shower off the bedroom. I turned on the water fully. There were ants in my hair, crawling around my eyes and ears but the water did a great job and I was soon rid of the ants and no great damage done. Back in the bedroom the place was crawling with thousands of them. In frustration I spewed a tin of aerosol at them. I couldn't believe the effect. Instantly from the thousands on the bed to the myriads in the room a signal was given. The very ones at the door coming in did an about-turn and within minutes the room was cleared save the few thousand dead ones caused by the aerosol.

Meeting an Olympic hero

On one of my travels in Tanganyika I was invited to stay at the home of Bob Tisdale. For non-sporting addicts I should point out that Bob Tisdale from Co. Tipperary was an Olympic gold medallist for Ireland in the 1932 Los Angeles Olympics. There he won the 400 metres hurdles. In his senior years he had bought a coffee farm in Tanganyika quite near the Ngorora game reserve. It was quite extensive. At night he had to hire local help to keep the elephants from invading and ruining his crop. It paid off in the end and he was able to retire to Australia.

Meeting someone like myself keen to hear his sporting stories, he spoke freely. He showed me his Olympic medal. When I asked to see some of the paper reports he told me that they were in a file which was stolen and lost.

He said proudly that Ireland fared well at the 1932 Olympics as another Irishman, Dr. Pat O'Callaghan from Cork won the gold medal for hammer throwing. Pat had been a brilliant medical graduate but was involved in much sport and won many medals. At the Olympic Games in Amsterdam in 1928, he won the gold medal for hammer throwing. Now four years later he was defending his title. He was trailing throughout the competition and Bob Tisdale spoke proudly of the help he was able to give him. Pat was wearing shoes with long spikes which were ill suited for the hard surface. Tisdale did some surgery on the shoes with hacksaw and file and made them more suitable for the hard ground. Although trailing till then, O'Callaghan unleashed an enormous effort on his final throw to grab victory, claim the gold medal and salute the tricolour once again. It was so pleasant to listen to Bob Tisdale recalling sporting events.

He eventually retired to Australia. When the Olympics were held in Sydney at the beginning of this century, it was discovered that Bob Tisdale was the oldest Olympic gold medallist. He was invited to present the medals to the winners of the 400 metres hurdles but declined the honour.

Chapter Sixteen

A Pilgrimage to Lourdes.

One of the most inspiring memories I have is of a pilgrimage to Marian Shrine at Lourdes in the presence of many sick people. Ordinarily the sight of so many people suffering from so many diseases and physical deformities can depress you. Not so in Lourdes. You are inspired by the example of so much courage and even joy in the midst of suffering. This courage puts many of us to shame when we start complaining about the minor irritants and discomforts of life. The sick at Lourdes may come praying for a cure. What they often get is a greater miracle, the grace to accept their crosses with courage and resignation. Their faith is strengthened and they get a vision of life in which suffering has a meaning. The many helpers at Lourdes are also inspiring. From the top medical professionals to those helping the sick in the wheelchairs, they are all voluntary and consider it a privilege to help.

However, there are miracles at Lourdes. On one visit there I was privileged to get access to the medical Bureau, not open to the public and to hear a lecture on the miracles that have taken place. In researching a cure only organic diseases are considered. There must be full medical tests and x-rays on the individual before and after the event. When the cure is reported there follows a long process of investigation by medical and other experts. There is great reluctance to declare a miracle until every natural explanation is excluded.

We were shown the records of one cure, that of an Italian soldier. His hip bone was entirely destroyed by cancer as the x-rays showed. He was taken to the baths where one is helped to shower and then with a prayer pushed into a tub of water. Afterwards in a wheel-chair he joined the Blessed Sacrament procession. He suddenly felt a surge of strength and stood up cured. He was rushed to the theatre. X-rays showed his hip bone totally restored. This case was so extraordinary that it attracted some three thousand specialists from all over the world to examine the records. They could find no explanation. The soldier in question later married at Lourdes and he and his bride spent their honeymoon tending the sick.

Mrs Feeley who was in charge of the medical Bureau at the time of my visit told us of her own cure. She had seven major operations because of a growth in the chest bone which was cancerous. She came to Lourdes praying for courage to cope with her illness and not to die empty handed. She was taken to the baths. Later at the Blessed Sacrament procession, she seemed to hear a voice telling her to go to the baths again. This time as she sank into the water she was completely cured.

In Lourdes there are up to two thousand patients there at any one time. When we think of the staff required to give proper care to those we wonder how this is possible. Yet the incredible fact is that all work done there is voluntary. There is an explosion of charity which is a miracle of a different sort. It is the many acts of kindness, multiplied a thousand-fold that make up the bouquets offered to Our Lady.

Countless people from many different countries come there to help and go away at the end inspired by the whole experience.

A visit to Lourdes is a strong invitation to ponder on the meaning of pain and suffering which are part and parcel of our life's journey and on the effect these have on one's character. Some philosophers tell us that most of our neuroses arise from our efforts to avoid pain. Ernest Hemmingway observes that while life breaks all of us in one way or another, some people grow at the broken places. Others become self-centred and pre-occupied with their problems.

Whenever I feel sorry for myself and my problems I think of Lourdes and especially of one patient whom I got to know quite well. She was a girl aged twenty-three, a polio victim, a stretcher case. I have never met a more cheerful person. In spite of her great pain she radiated a sense of serenity and happiness. Her interests were wide, her questions were about other people, about me and my missionary work. *"But what about you?"* I asked. She smiled and said, *"I would appreciate a little prayer, as I'm going to have two operations when I get back home. If they are successful, I'll be able to sit up and even get into a wheel-chair. Won't that be great?"* I returned to talk to her several times. The effect was always the same. The triumph of her spirit over the chains of pain and sickness gave one a great uplift of the soul and courage to face one's problems whether big or small.

Some facts about Lourdes

There are countless cures of emotional and psychological nature, of people coping with alcohol and other addictions, but these are not listed in the Medical Bureau. Only organic cures with full medical records before and after the cure are listed. At the time of my visit, there were sixty five miracles registered.

The baths used by so many people are obviously not free from bacteria and other pollutants. Yet there is no record of anyone contracting a disease from the baths. There is no record of anyone dying later from the illness cured at Lourdes

It is interesting that Our Lady never mentioned about physical healing. Bernadette died young. When it was suggested that she should return to Lourdes, she declared that the water of Lourdes was not for her.

Chapter Seventeen

A story of Reconciliation

One of the great consolations of our Christian faith is the fact that the God we worship is a God of infinite mercy and compassion. Reconciliation sums up the whole of Christ's ministry, union with God and with each other. Forgiveness is always there for us provided we are sorry and amend our lives and fulfil one other vital obligation, the need to forgive others. It is the one petition in the Our Father with a condition attached. It is the acid test of our Christian faith, to forgive others unconditionally just as we ask God for forgiveness. It has to do with my own mental attitude. It does not mean forgetting or allowing the perpetrator to go free.

Let me tell a story from our own tragic history which illustrates this point beautifully. On the 6th May, 1882, Lord Frederick Cavendish, the British Secretary of State for Ireland and his secretary, Thomas Burke were butchered to death inside the gates of the Phoenix Park in Dublin. It was a particularly brutal murder. The perpetrators were called the Invincibles, a group of militant Republicans anxious to set Ireland free by violent means. They were rounded up and charged but nobody would give evidence against them until one of their own members was bribed to turn informer. In return for a free pardon he swore away the lives of his fellow-conspirators. On his evidence they were found guilty and sentenced to be hanged.

Awaiting execution they were visited in prison by a kindly chaplain and all made their peace with God, all except one man called Joe Brady who had led the attack. It was not because of lack of faith. In fact there was a certain amount of rugged integrity about the man. When *he refused to go to confession to the chaplain he said openly: "Look, I know I committed a terrible crime. I murdered Lord Cavendish and Thomas Burke. For that I am sorry before God."* The chaplain asked him, *"Then why don't you want to go to confession and receive sacramental absolution?"* Brady answered, *"Because there is one person I cannot and will not forgive, that informer who sold our lives for the price of his own. In confession we ask God for forgiveness just as we forgive others. I'm no hypocrite. So what's the use?"* Brady remained like that till the night before his execution. On that night a nun came and asked to see the condemned man. She was ushered into his cell. Brady looked at her in amazement. He said, *"Sister, what do you want? Please leave me alone."* The nun said simply, *"I need your help. I have a question to ask and I want an honest answer. I think someone about to die will give me an honest answer."*

Brady said simply, *"That I will do, Sister, what is your question?"*

The nun said, *"For some time now I have been consumed with hatred for one individual. I cannot seem to get over it. Because of it, I feel a hypocrite leading the religious life. I feel I should leave the convent. What would you advise?"*

Brady paused and then in his simple direct way said, *"Sister, you above all, should be able to find it in your heart to forgive this person, whoever he or she is, whatever has been done to you, and remain a nun. That is my advice to you."*

The nun looked at him for a long time and then said slowly, *"Very well, Mr. Brady, I'll take your advice and because of what you said, from the bottom of my heart, I forgive you for murdering my brother, Thomas Burke."* It was a dramatic moment and then Joe Brady realised what forgiveness was all about. He realised that this nun, whose brother he had killed, could easily have sat at home, taking a grim satisfaction knowing the man who had murdered her brother was about to receive his just desserts and good riddance and who cares. But she cared. Perhaps she did feel revulsion against him. But she sought him out and told him she forgave him. Joe Brady begged the nun's forgiveness. Better still, he went to confession. He was reconciled to both God and man when he met his death the following morning.

Chapter Eighteen

An inspiring tale from Derry

For many years people were saddened by the atrocities committed in Derry such as the events of Bloody Sunday. Thankfully there are stories of heroism and forgiveness too. Here is a tale which inspired people. It even attracted the attention of the Dalai Lama, leader of Tibetan Buddhism, who had received the Nobel Peace Prize and who came specially to meet the man in question and to say to him, "You are my hero."

Richard Moore had been blinded by a rubber bullet many years before. Rather than dwell on his misfortune he founded the charity *Children in Crossfire*. The Dalai Lama came to the tenth anniversary celebration to express his support.

Richard Moore was ten when a British soldier fired a rubber bullet at him at close range when he was on his way home from school. This happened in 1997. With incredible courage and with help from friends he founded the charity *Children in Crossfire* to help other victims.

When the charity was celebrating its tenth anniversary, Richard spoke to more than a thousand people in Derry's Millennium Forum. He said he had always a desire to meet the soldier who blinded him. With the help of a BBC TV crew he managed to track down the soldier and wrote him a letter. They met and Richard told the soldier that he forgave him completely and invited him to come to Derry anonymously for the anniversary celebrations.

However the Dalai Lama had come for the occasion too and quietly arranged for the soldier to come on stage and be introduced. In an unforgettable scene the three men embraced. Addressing the crowd the soldier said that for many years he had felt devastated by the knowledge that he had caused Richard's blindness. He described the letter from Richard as one of the most inspiring he had ever received, *"When we met, we were like long lost brothers. We have gone from strength to strength since then. This man is a great friend to me. If Richard and I can do this, there's hope for the country and everyone in it."*

Another man who inspires us as we read his story is **Nelson Mandela.** After more than twenty years in prison under the apartheid regime in South Africa he emerged from the long harsh treatment with no bitterness and with a great desire to unite all the people in a free South Africa. He is truly one of the greatest African leaders. What sustained him in prison? Many things but the following poem always gave him the courage to continue:

INVICTUS by William Ernest Henley

Out of the night that covers me
Black as the pit from pole to pole
I thank whatever gods may be
For my unconquerable soul.

In the full clutch of circumstance
I have not winced nor cried aloud.
Under the bludgeoning of chance
My head is bloody but unbowed.

Beyond this place of wrath and tears
Lies but the horror of the shade,
And yet the menace of the years
Finds and shall find me unafraid.

It matters not how strait the gate,
How charged with punishments the scroll,
I am the master of my fate,
I am the captain of my soul.

Chapter Nineteen

Do you believe in ghosts

New York State is a beautiful county and the Catskill area is a favourite vacation spot, being mountainous, cool and covered with trees. East Durham is one such holiday resort and I had some pleasant times there with my brother Mike and his family. There's a small church nearby where I could say Mass. On one occasion a priest from a nearby holiday village came and asked me to supply for him the following weekend as he wanted to get away for a family function. I accepted.

I was there in good time on the Saturday evening and a lady claiming she was the housekeeper and general factotum showed me around. There was a small wooden house beside the church where I could stay if I wished. However there was no electricity and the only light was a battery powered torch in the small bed-sitter. The nosey housekeeper asked me a lot of questions including one about ghosts and did I believe in them as there were stories around. I was non-committal. If I didn't want to stay in the house, there was accommodation in a hostelry down the road and she would book me a room if I wished. I told her I would decide when I had looked around. She told me with a touch of warning that the last priest who stayed in the house left it in the middle of the night to go to the hostel.

I went to have a look at the house. It was fairly dilapidated but at least there was a toilet and the one bed had clean sheets. There was an armchair beside the bed and on a small side table the lamp stood, battery powered and heavy. I strolled around outside and I noticed a small graveyard nearby. One grave was that of a two year old girl tragically killed in an accident some years before.

I then went to the hostelry pondering if I should stay there for the night. I found it rather noisy and a group was organising a disco which would continue late into the night. I strolled back to the house. There was no lock on the door which was damaged and the holes were covered with mesh wire. I found the armchair comfortable enough and I sat down and relaxed. I dozed off and was surprised when I woke up to find the place in darkness.

Then I heard the first sound of tap tap tap. It sounded like the gentle steps of a child waking outside my door. I must be dreaming. No, the sound continued and seemed to move into the kitchen. Then I heard a flutter of steps. I stood up, opened the door but could see nothing. I couldn't move the heavy lamp so I closed the door, sat down again and listened. It was eerie. There was some noise outside and it resembled the sound of a baby crying. It must be the wind. I remember the housekeeper asking about ghosts. I'm not a scary person so I sat and waited. I heard the gentle padded steps again. Eventually tiredness took over and I fell asleep in the armchair. When I woke up, the morning light greeted me. Tiredly I undressed and rolled into the bed for another couple of hours sleep. I was wakened by the housekeeper knocking on the window. She had promised to bring me a morning coffee.

She looked around the room and asked me if I slept well. She told me the last priest who stayed there ran out of the house and down to the hostelry in the middle of the night when he heard some steps outside his door. Did I not hear them? Then she added, *"I should have warned you. The house is full of squirrels!"*

Ghost stories were a great feature of nightly conversation in rural Ireland when I was young. In pre-T.V. days they provided great entertainment and many believed ghosts existed. I loved the answer of the sceptical Kerryman when asked if he believed in them, as he said, *"No, but they're there alright."* How do ghost stories originate?

Once when I was in charge of the students in St. Joseph's, Freshford, I was reading in my office very late one night when I heard the sound of steps racing along the corridor to my room. A loud knock-knock on the door and I shouted, *"come in,"* and there stood one of the junior students, Noel Healy, literally with his hair standing on his head. He cried out, *"Father, help me. I woke up and there was a ghost lepping on my bed."* I calmed him down and asked what happened. He was in the infirmary room, all alone, as he had been sick. Normally a senior boy should be there too. Noel woke up and saw a huge hand trying to grasp him. He jumped up and ran out the door and headed for my room. He was lucky I was still up. After a while I took him back to the infirmary room, gathered up his sheets and blankets and brought him up to the boys dormitory, tucked him into his old bed and told him he'd be safe now with some thirty boys around him.

I went back to the infirmary room and sat there for a while wondering what caused the scare. Then I had an idea. I switched off the light and waited in the dark. Then I saw what had happened. The moon came out from behind clouds and was shining in the window. A gentle breeze caused a movement in the branches of a tree outside which cast shadows inside. One such shadow was in the shape of a mighty hand and was moving up and down above the bed. Poor Noel woke from sleep and thought it was a ghost and ran for help.

A genuine visitor

While most ghost stories have their origin in strange happenings, yet if we accept the apparitions at Lourdes, Fatima or Knock, we have to accept the possibility of the departed communicating with us. I once met a very credible witness who told me her story. She was very ill in hospital, worried about recovery. She had a room to herself and one afternoon was reading a spiritual book when a gentleman entered. He seemed to be a doctor but was not on the staff of the hospital as she did not recognise him. He spoke kindly to her, assured her that she would recover and to continue her apostolate of teaching Sacred Scripture as it was very important. Some time after he left, the ward sister came in and the patient asked who her visitor was. The ward sister smiled and assured her that she had no visitor. She had been on duty all afternoon and nobody had passed her desk. It must be all a dream. The patient said, *"certainly not. I was wide awake reading when he came in and assured me so wonderfully. His presence was a God-send."* There the matter might have ended but some time later when the patient recovered, she recognised her visitor after seeing a picture of him. He was Maximilian Kolbe, the famous martyr from Auschwitz.

Psychic foresight

There are many stories of omens and portents of future events but here is one that can be verified. It concerns a Religious Sister living in community in Uganda.

On one Monday morning she woke up very distressed. She had seen her younger sister who had qualified as a doctor and was now working in an Irish hospital, drown in a dreadful accident. Her fellow sisters told her it was just a bad dream but she continued to worry so much that she decided to ring her mother in Limerick. These were bad days in Uganda and it took her a couple of hours to get through. Her mother was surprised. *"Was my sister home at the week-end? Was she driving? Did she get back to the hospital safely? Did you talk to her this morning, etc.?"* Her mother assured that she had spoken on the phone to her just a few minutes before. She was fine. So what was the worry about? Relief all round. The sister and community in Uganda were all happy. Just a bad dream!

Or was it? Two weeks later, her sister in Ireland drowned in exactly the circumstances as seen in the dream. This led to awful mental anxiety and confusion. Could she have saved her sister? Life is a mystery.

Sister Death

I am a wealthy merchant in Iraq. This morning one of my servants asked for time off as he had some shopping to do in the nearby trading centre. He departed cheerfully but an hour later came back in considerable distress, *"Master, please help me. I was doing my shopping and then round a corner I met sister death. She made a threatening gesture at me. Master, I must get away. If you lend me your fastest steed, I can reach Aleppo by sundown. I have friends there so I shall be safe,"*

He took my horse and galloped away at considerable speed.

This afternoon out of curiosity I went to the trading centre and looked around. Sure enough, behind a screen, I saw sister death. I accosted her. *"Why did you make a threatening gesture at my servant this morning?"* She replied quietly. *"That was not a threatening gesture. It was an expression of surprise. I was amazed to see him here at this centre because I have an appointment to meet in Aleppo at sundown."*

Chapter Twenty

The Irish Diaspora

Emigration was always a feature of late Irish history but what caused massive emigration was the famine of 1847-48. In a few years the population of Ireland dropped from roughly eight million to four million. Many went to Britain to find work and to send money back home to support their families. The vast majority however, countless thousands, risked the dreadful conditions of steerage in the ships to America. From 1850 to 1930 Irish emigration to America totalled almost four million.

Although the vast majority came from a rural background, they settled in the cities mostly on the east coast of America. They had two advantages over other immigrants from Europe. They spoke English and from Irish history, especially from the work of Daniel O'Connell, they had a good grasp of how politics works. They came together, organised pressure groups and picked clever leaders. Tammany Hall was the result. The Irish got a grip on big city government that could look after the welfare of newcomers from Ireland and promote members to important positions. They were overwhelmingly members of the Democratic party. A good example of the power of politics was Mayor Richard Daley of Chicago. He had vast influence and was sometimes accused of ballot-stuffing. He was certainly responsible for winning the state of Illinois for John F. Kennedy which was crucial in Kennedy's election victory.

All this had a great influence of what was happening back in Ireland. Most Irish in America had a bitter hatred of Britain, especially because of its lack of help during the famine period. Some called that neglect genocide. They gave full support to any movement in Ireland which promoted independence even through armed struggle. They would back it every way they could, especially financially.

So Britain now had to cope with a powerful, implacable and influential enemy within a country which was growing in world importance. And nationalists in Ireland had a fruitful source of money, guns and propaganda. They would soon make their presence felt.

Emigration to other countries

The Irish who emigrated to Britain did so to find jobs and provide for their families. They were not active politically. Their presence there was a great boost to the Catholic Church and many religious vocations came from Irish families.

Some Irish were banished to the wilds of **Australia** as punishment for so-called misdemeanours. I have added a short article on the success of some of them. See *Dead men walking*. But by and large Australia was considered too far away and did not attract many Irish emigrants although three of my uncles went there. One remained there and married and some of his family contacted me recently.

A very interesting part of the emigration story is the number of people who went to **Argentina.** In the eighteen seventies, six of my grand-parent's family went there, four sons including my father and two daughters. I have written about them in my other book and the following article fills in more details.

The Irish in Argentina

There is a strong Irish community in Argentina, the majority descended from emigrants from the Westmeath/Longford area. They are very proud of their Celtic roots and Catholic faith. The connection goes back to early 19th Century. Argentina won independence from Spain in 1816. Admiral William Brown was from Foxford, Co. Mayo. He is honoured as the founder of the Argentine navy. Another man too, Thomas O'Brien from Co. Wicklow, was adjutant to San Martin, the hero of the war of Independence. It is said that San Martin, begged O'Brien to bring out people from Ireland to develop Argentina, a country of vast unclaimed lands.

O'Brien came to Ireland, no success in Wicklow. Then he met John Mooney of Streamstown, Co. Westmeath. His sister, Mary, was married to Patrick Bookey, and the three of them accompanied O'Brien when he returned to Argentina in 1828. They achieved rapid success in farming and wrote home to Ireland, telling of the great opportunities and begging people to come out. This was the beginning of the great exodus from Westmeath/Longford to Argentina. A small percentage also arrived from Wexford, Cork and Clare and some other counties. Soon the names of Murray, Geoghegan, Kenny, Nugent, Moran and Brown, were as common out there as at home.

After the famine in Ireland, one man, Fr. Antonio Fahy, a Dominican priest from Co. Galway, played a huge role in bringing Irish people to Argentina. He urged them: *"Come to Argentina: You are from the land; here there's land for the taking."* He was organiser, banker, adviser, matchmaker - highly respected. He played a prominent role in catering for the welfare of the immigrant Irish. His memory is greatly revered.

My own family connection with Argentina began in 1865 when my oldest uncle, Alexander, emigrated there at the age of 18. In all, 6 of my grandparent's children went to Argentina including my father, Michael Fox. He went there in 1877 with his brother, Owen (Eugene). His passage was paid on a tramp steamer from Liverpool to Buenos Aires. Dad had three sovereigns in his pocket. On arrival he worked for a farmer, the idea being to save and buy his own place. In fact Alexander became a very successful sheep-rancher and Owen a cattle rancher.

After 10 years, in 1887, Dad was thinking of a trip to Ireland and counting the cost, but then a great opportunity presented itself. The famous showman, Buffalo Bill, William Cody, was taking his Wild West show through S. America to Europe. He wanted to show Europe what the old Wild West was all about. He had many cowboys, Pony Express outriders and some 150 Indians, including Sitting Bull, the great Chief who had conquered General Custer at the famous battle of Little Big Horn a few years previously. Part of the show was the re-enactment of the famous battle. Dad saw the opportunity, joined up as a participant and was with the show till its final night at the famous London arena, Earls Court. On the last night of the show, Cody himself called Dad to say goodbye. He said to him: *"I know you're leaving us to visit your family in Ireland. No need to work tonight. Have a seat in my box and enjoy the show. Good luck."*

Dad spent the Summer in Ireland and returned to Argentina later that year. He continued his work there. He was best man at his brother Eugene's (Owen's) wedding to Catherine Tobin in 1898. The following year, Thomas, the second eldest son, who was running the farm back in Killeenbrack, Westmeath, died suddenly. Dad was invited home to take his place. He returned to Ireland for good in 1901 and settled down on the farm. He married Brigid Scally in 1906. They had three children, Owen, Ellen and Alexander. Sadly she died in 1911 after the birth of her third child. Seven years later at the age of 59, Dad married my mother, Mary Jane Mulvany, on June 5th 1918. They had six children, of which I happen to be the youngest, born when Dad was 72 and Mum was 42. But that's another story - and a long one!

Chapter Twenty one

Dead men walking

I love that beautiful ballad *The Fields of Athenry* wherein a young mother laments the deportation of her husband, *"because you stole Trevelyan's corn that the young might see the morn. Now a prison ship lies waiting in the bay."*
It refers to a tragic period in Irish history, a time of rack-rents by cruel landlords and families thrown out of their humble homes because they couldn't pay the unjust rent. Many men were deported to the wilds of Australia. Some were imprisoned in Tasmania. Many escaped but never made it back to Ireland. However from this sad period there is an inspiring tale.

Nine men were captured, tried and convicted of treason in what has been referred to as "Young Irish Disorders" shortly after the great famine of 1847-48. The nine who were sentenced to death were Pat Donoghue, Charles Duffy, Michael Ireland, Morris Lyene, Thomas McGee, Terence McManus, Thomas Meagher, John Mitchell and Richard O'Gorman.

The judge asked if there was anything any of them wanted to say before being sentenced. Meagher whose attitude summed up the attitude of them all replied: *"My Lord, this is our first offence but not our last. If you will be easy with us this once, we promise on our word as gentlemen, to do better next time, sure we won't be fools to get caught."*

The judge, outraged rather than amused at Meagher's remarks, indignantly decreed that they should be hanged until dead, then drawn and quartered. Passionate protests, however, influenced Queen Victoria to commute the sentence to banishment for life and transportation to far wild Australia.

In 1874 an astounded Queen Victoria received word that Sir Charles Duffy who had been elected as Prime Minister of Australia was the very same Charles Duffy who had been transported some twenty five years before. Curious about the fate of the other eight the Queen demanded the records of those transported in 1848 to be researched and revealed. This was what was found:

Thomas Meagher - Governor of Montana
Terence McManus - Brigadier General U.S. Army
Patrick Donoghue - Brigadier General U.S. Army
Richard O'Gorman - Governor of Newfoundland.
Maurice Lyene - Attorney General of Australia
Michael Ireland - Attorney General of Australia (after Lyene)

Chapter Twenty two

A critical view of the Church

We missionaries were sometimes offered a chance to take time out and do a Sabbatical year, a time for reflection and study. It came in the wake of the second Vatican Council which introduced many changes in the Church as regards liturgy and practice. Many church doctrines were examined carefully again in the light of new developments in Scripture study and science. Galileo, a great astronomer and mathematician, unjustly condemned for his teaching on the solar system was one example of the Church's need to update its teaching in the light of modern research.

I was privileged to be given the opportunity of doing a sabbatical year in Rome, where I stayed at our house and attended various courses on theology and mission work. It was very fulfilling. At weekends I had time to visit the many magnificent sights in this wonderful city.

Our house is about half an hour's walk from the Vatican. From the top of the Geniculum hill there is a panoramic view of the city. I often stopped to admire the scene. I would cast my mind back two thousand years and picture the events happening at that time. I could see triumphant soldiers parading home from the Gallic wars, their captives and their booty in tow. I imagined the great Forum centre of brilliant debate and issuing laws and I could see Nero's palace glistening in the morning sun.

Then, in my mind's eye, I see a wondering stranger finding his way to the city, possibly under cover of darkness and with his few possessions in a string bag. He is Peter the Fisherman, coming to Rome to make contact with the few Christians there and to take charge of the group. He worked tirelessly for some years under persecution, was caught, crucified upside down and buried in an unmarked grave. Was he dead and forgotten?

Now as I look, the conquests of Rome are forgotten, the Forum is but a pile of ruins, Nero's palace has disappeared but in the heart of this great city, on Sunday next the successor of St. Peter will address almost a million pilgrims from all over the world, proclaiming the Good news of the Gospel, that Christ has died, Christ has risen, Christ will come again. One could not but feel proud to belong to this worldwide Catholic Church. It was a privilege to promote its message of reconciliation, love of God and love of our neighbour, irrespective of age, colour or ethnic background. That is the image of the Church that has kept me going throughout my missionary years.

Another image

There is of course another image which has to be faced and one should not be afraid to face reality. I have just been perusing a book entitled **Papal Sin.** It is by Garry Wills, an American academic and it does not make for easy reading. It is not anti-Church but it highlights the chequered history of the Papacy and Church leaders down the years. In our own time we have been blest with great leaders but it was not always so. There have been bad Popes and many scandals in Church circles down the years. In a way it is indirectly a pointer to the Church's divine origin. Otherwise it would have collapsed long ago. Jesus has warned us to be prepared. In Matthew's gospel in chapter thirteen He speaks of the Kingdom of heaven as a field where good seed was sown but an enemy came at night and planted weeds among the wheat.

The Church is the body of Christ, made up of human members and it has all the strengths and weaknesses that that entails. It has nourished saints and it has inspired countless acts of goodness and heroism in every age. It has also sheltered great sinners and caused many scandals. It is easy to point these out, but the Gospel is an invitation to look into our own hearts and souls and see what is there. The great Russian author, Alexander Solzhenitsyn, who saw so much evil in the Russian gulag, reminds us that the thin line between good and evil runs through every human heart. God gave us the precious gift of free will and it can be used for good or abused for evil. The different manifestations of evil weeds that can grow in our lives are often listed as the seven deadly sins. Do you remember them from your catechism lessons, pride, covetousness, lust, anger, gluttony, envy and sloth? These weeds can grow in different shapes and sizes in different people. Sometimes they seem to take over the whole field. Money, power or lust can become gods and enslave people. Jesus invites us to look into our minds and hearts, but not to be afraid because He is with us.

The Church too is a mysterious mixture of the divine and the human, of grace and free will, of divine seed sown in frail human soil. We can't expect a perfect crop. The Church is the Body of Christ and deserves our loyalty and love. But just as we look into our own hearts with honesty, we must also look into the Church with a sharp critical eye. We can see plenty of weeds there, not just the great betrayals and scandals but also the foolish ecclesiastical posturing and clerical careerism.

There is no doubt that the greatest scandal to hit the Church in recent times is clerical sexual abuse of minors. We saw the evil of the abuse itself but also the cover-up by Church officials to protect the perpetrators and the image of the Church. There was a lot of ignorance involved, as regards the deep damage done to victims and the hope that counselling or a change of scene might cure the perpetrator. It is an evil addiction and hard to overcome. Personally I was upset and stunned when I read some of the reports as I knew some of those involved. The Church has a lot to do to repair the damage.

Some members left the Church because of the scandals. This is understandable but a pity. Jesus tells us that we are meant to be a leaven helping the growth of the Church and the good of all members. The Church is what its members make it. We may be shocked at times but we do not turn away but renew our efforts at renewal. I love the quote of Carlo Corretto, a great Italian spiritual writer, which neatly reflects the attitude of concerned Christians. He addresses the Church in these words: *How much I must criticise you my Church and yet how much I love you. You have made me suffer more than anyone and yet I owe you more than I owe anyone. You have given me much scandal and yet you alone have made me understand holiness. Never in the world have I seen anything more compromised, more false, yet never have I touched anything more pure, more generous or more beautiful. Countless times I have felt like slamming the door of my soul in your face. And yet, every night I have prayed that I might die in your arms.*

Chapter Twenty three

The wealth of the Catholic Church

The Church has lost a lot of credibility because of clerical sex abuse which has to be condemned forcefully and avoided at all costs. But the scandal should not take away from the enormous humanitarian work of the Church through the world. Below are some statistics which I have taken from an article some time ago. But the picture is the same today perhaps enriched by increased donations.

- The annual operating budget of the Vatican is about €220 million, a bit less than the Irish dept. of foreign affairs.
- The Vatican's budget is €175 million, less than the Irish Gov. dept. of Arts, Sports and wildlife.
- In 2004, the Vatican's assets, land, buildings, investments, etc. were worth about €660 million (Trinity Colleges similar assets in 2008 were given at 650 million.)

What about the art treasures of the Vatican which are not included. These constitute a treasury for all humanity; they cannot be sold or borrowed against. They cost millions to maintain. Should the Irish Government sell the Ardagh

Chalice or the Book of Kells to subsidise say, the Health service?

The Vatican is run on a shoe string. **Yet the Church is one of the great forces for humanitarian work throughout the world. With over 625,000 volunteers, it directly helped 25 million people in over 200 countries last year.**

This is not all. Aids became a huge problem in seventies.

- At that time in Africa 27% of all victims are being treated in Catholic hospitals.
- In India, though Catholics are a tiny minority, they run 5,500 health care institutions.
- Every year the Vatican gives to 3rd world countries twice as much as Bob Geldolf raised in his great Band Aid project.
- Mission (Pontifical Mission Societies) worldwide supports 194,855 schools, 5,246 hospitals, 17,530 dispensaries, 577 leprosy centres and 80,560 social and pastoral centres.
- In areas of human tragedy, such as the earthquake in Haiti, Caritas (the Catholic Relief Agency) is always first in the field to offer help.
- Aid to the Church in Need distributed over 65 million euro in aid in 2010.
- Catholic Aid agencies such as Trocaire, Concern, Goal & Cafod distribute several million worth of aid in the most distressed parts of the world every year.

This is the Church we are proud to belong to. It is made up of human members with all the strengths and weaknesses that that implies. It has nurtured countless heroes and heroines, even if it has sheltered some awful sinners. For all its faults, it continues to inspire its members to self-sacrifice, generosity and heroism. I have yet to see a hospital or dispensary or clinic for the poor run by an atheistic or humanist society.

Chapter Twenty four

Careerism in the Church

When members of our Society made their final commitment to serve on the missions we each received a red sash which we wore proudly every day. It was a symbol of one's willingness to die for Christ. We were ordained at Mill Hill in London. After ordination I attended a funeral in Ireland with some diocesan priests and I wore my red sash. When we gathered in the sacristy afterwards an old priest came over to me and said, *"young man, where did you get that sash?"* I was in the process of explaining it as a Society symbol when he cut me short and pointing to some of his old colleagues around him said, *"some of these old fogies would give anything for a thing like that."* He was referring to its use when it was part of the investiture when one was made a monsignor, a rare event among Irish diocesan priests. I didn't wear my red sash again on such occasions.

In some countries many priests sought honour and rank in their clerical career. Undoubtedly many of them deserved it, having done great pastoral work for many years. But sometimes it got a bit out of hand. When some bishops from the United States went to Rome on official visits, they were expected to bring back authority to confer the title of Monsignor on quite a few of their priests. I was working in Albany when I heard that one local pastor was so honoured so I dropped in to greet him. I was amazed at the set-up. Not only was he wearing all his purple robes, sash and all, but inside the front door a second set of robes hung on a clothes-horse and when one opened the door a spotlight shone on the lot. I couldn't help feeling that we had come a long way from the poor man of Nazareth.

The dark side of all this is the problem of careerism in the church. Over the years clerics took on the trappings of power and made sure their attire gave evidence of that power. Popes were not averse to this display of importance. I still remember Pope Paul the sixth being carried majestically on the sede gestatoria and wearing the papal tiara. Fortunately he soon gave up the practice. There is a well known shop in Rome called Gamorelli which supplies clerical outfits to match any clerical position of importance. Once I was based in Rome for a sabbatical year of study so I often had a chance to stroll around the magnificent city and often passed the shop. I sometimes watched ambitious young clerics from all round the globe doing their buying of clerical purple.

In the Vatican itself and in the Curia, the governing body of the Church, are many capable and excellent men, but knowing some of them, one felt there was always a struggle for power and promotion. Many of them have little pastoral experience of working with the poor and needy, but they still believe that they rule the Church and know what's best for all of us. Fortunately at present we have a wonderful Pope who is trying to change all this.

Careerism in the Church is totally wrong. While many ecclesiastics are excellent and deserve their position by their ability and holiness, yet others, less worthy strut around showing off their power. It's about time they had a sense of their own unimportance. They should remember that their lives should be centred on the Man from Nazareth whose life's journey led to utter humiliation and death among criminals. To be occupied with climbing the pyramid of power and prestige is surely a denial of all that Jesus stood for and puts many people off from embracing the Church. Status seeking and the cult of celebrity is the essence of worldly values.

Chapter Twenty five

Are you saved?

In Jesus Christ the whole of the human race is saved because He died for all of us. Salvation is a free gift of God Like every gift it has to be accepted by us by professing our faith in Jesus and living according to his teaching of love and reconciliation. Certainly I am saved in so far as Jesus is my Saviour. But salvation is a life-long process. We must persevere to the end in living according to the Gospel or if we fail along the way, repent and make amends. We have no guarantee of salvation other than our faith in Jesus Christ.

When I worked in Uganda, at one stage there was a big movement called the Saved Ones. They believed that if you knew a bit of S. Scripture and kept repeating it you were saved, irrespective of the sort of life you lived. The movement attracted many people and they challenged individuals. I met a group of them one day and they boldly asked me, *"you sir, are you saved?"* I answered with a smile, *"No my friends, and I've got news for you too. You're not saved either. But I hope we are all on the road to salvation through our faith in Jesus Christ and living according to his teaching, as St. Paul reminds us in his letter to the Philippians."*

I have not yet won but I am still running, trying to capture the prize for which Christ Jesus captured me. I assure you my brothers that I am far from thinking that I

have already won. All I can say is that I forget the past and I strain ahead for what is still to come. I am racing for the finish to which God calls me upwards to receive in Christ Jesus. **(Philippians 3 12-15)**

To be saved we are called upon to live a life of integrity.

In our reading of Scripture Adam is the personification of every man. His story is the story of us all. We are living in a world of incredible goodness and dreadful evil. Our struggle is the struggle for integrity. The whole of human history has been the story of our combat with the powers of evil stretching from the dawn of history until the last day. Finding himself in the midst of the battlefield, man has to struggle to do what is right. It is often at great cost to himself but aided by God's grace he can succeed in achieving his own inner integrity. Man and woman face many temptations in life, to cheat, to cut corners, to have an affair, excusing oneself that everybody is doing it and the commandments are old hat anyway!

The struggle for integrity is part of the human condition. Jesus being fully human had to face that struggle. The three temptations described in Matthew's Gospel represent all our temptations.

We long for the fleshpots of Egypt and are tempted to do anything to amass wealth but Jesus reminds to that there is a deeper spiritual yearning in our hearts and minds.

The temptation to fame, power and glory, are part of the human condition and some people are ready to pay a heavy price for a mere bubble of honour. Think of the abuse of drugs in the sporting world.

Lastly whatever takes the place of God in our lives is a false god. We must get our priorities right and not be deceived by attractive illusions which soon prove false.

It is easy to see the effects of original sin all around us. Just look at the headlines in the daily tabloids. But we must also be aware of the power of Christ's grace working within us and we see so much goodness and love in the lives of many wonderful men and women.

Chapter Twenty Six

The challenges that young people face

Let me begin with a quote: "*Young people now love luxury. They have bad manners, contempt for authority. They have become tyrants in the household. They contradict their elders and tyrannise their parents.*"
This was written not by some angry parent or teacher of today, but by the Greek philosopher, Socrates, writing 400 years B.C. It shows that in some ways times haven't changed a great deal. Each generation grows up, often rebels against established customs and are blamed for not conforming.

Human nature doesn't change. What does change, however, are the pressures and influences of a given time. I like the response of the young lad in reply to his dad who said to him, "*Now son, when I was your age…*" his son replied "*Dad, you were never my age…*" Old folks never had to face the challenges of today's generation.

When I was young, drink and drugs were no great problems, simply because they were not available and besides, there was little money around. Neither were we exposed to the scenes of violence and mayhem as seen today on our T.V. and depicted on the tabloids. The pressures on young people today are vastly different but certain truths should be kept in mind.

1. The values which have the greatest influence on young people are the values they see practised in their own homes by parents and elders. The home remains the primary educational centre.

2. We should remember Fr. Flanagan, the founder of Boystown and his claim that there is no such thing as a bad boy or girl. An Irish priest working in America, he was an idealist but also a down-to-earth realist who had met and rehabilitated some of the toughest kids of his day. He meant that no one was so bad that there was not some good in him and if we could find and draw this element of good to the surface, we have something to build on. The success of Boystown proved that. When he visited Ireland he was highly critical of the harsh treatment given to the boys and girls in our care homes. Rather than listen to him, he was attacked by a deputy in Dail Eireann for giving Ireland a bad name.

3. In treating young people a word of praise is of more value than a thousand condemnations. This is an important lesson for parents, teachers or any of us who can be so quick to condemn at times. I once heard this advice given to teachers: *"If a kid in your school seems hopeless and the only thing he seems good at is driving nails, then for heaven's sake, will you once in a while, have a nail-driving competition."*

4. In general young people are generous and idealistic. With the right challenges before them and with inspiring examples they will respond and give of their best.

There are plenty of examples of this where young people have proved themselves. To see the many young people helping the sick at Lourdes is one inspiring example.

Chapter Twenty seven

Celtic Christian Spirituality

St. Patrick is the revered Apostle of Ireland. There were some Christians there before him but his was the dominant presence as a missionary. There are many legends about him but the outline of his life is fairly clear. Captured as a young man on the coast of Britain he spent years as a slave before he escaped. Later as a priest, as he tells us in his Confessions, he heard the voice of the Irish inviting him to come back and walk once more with them.

As a missionary he had the great advantage of knowing the language and the culture. He built on that. He took what was best in the Celtic pagan culture and he reaffirmed it and reframed it in terms of the Christian Gospel. People came to accept Christianity not as a rejection of their prior beliefs but as the fulfilment and completion of them. A very simple example of this is the Celtic Cross. Lovers of nature, some Celts worshipped the greatest symbol of nature, the sun. Patrick didn't just condemn this as superstition. He reminded the people that the sun was also part of God's creation and should remind all people of Christ, the light of the world. He stamped the Cross on the sun. In my ministry I was privileged to officiate at many weddings and very often my gift to the bride was the Celtic Cross.

Ireland after the famine was in dire straights. It had lost its nationhood, it had its language. The Catholic Church, though poor, led a remarkable revival, mainly through its parish structure, a priest, a church and a school. Later on the Church in Ireland became very dominant and was guilty of faults and cover-ups but it deserves great credit for this revival. It produced many outstanding priests.

In the second half of the 17th century in Europe a very unhealthy development took place in the Church. It was called **Jansenism.** Cornelis Jansen was a Flemish bishop who preached a very rigid form of Christianity, very much based on the dualistic principle, spirit versus body, earthly versus heavenly, material things and man's body were a source of evil. Christ did not die for all. The movement had a wide influence and led to rigid form of asceticism. It was condemned by the Church.

The counter-reformation after the Council of Trent led to a highly structured disciplined Church.

Unfortunately there was a multiplication of sanctions and an endless enumeration of sins both mortal and venial. This led to an unhealthy image of God and a religion dominated by obligation and fear rather than by love and celebration.

Sexual sins were seen as the worst sins in the book. A woman becoming pregnant outside of marriage was ostracised, often denounced from the altar. A woman entering the convent was seen *as leaving the world.* If a novice were allowed a rare visit home she was not allowed to enter the parental home, as if it were some sort of place of dubious repute!

Sins and sanctions were multiplied. To break the Friday fast (from meat) was a mortal sin. (just imagine: equated with murder and adultery!) All this teaching left a lot of worries and unnecessary feelings of guilt. We must thank God for the basic common sense of ordinary men and women who survived all this. But many devout people had psychological scars and feelings of guilt. Quite often in my priestly ministry I helped to heal those scars. There was great need of renewal and pastoral understanding of Church practice and, Thank God, this came about under Pope John XXIII and the Second Vatican Council.

Images play a powerful part in all relationships. If my image of God is that of a stern judge or policeman, rather than that of a loving Father as revealed by Jesus in the New Testament, then this negative image will affect my whole spirituality.

Celtic spirituality keeps us on the right path and is perfectly in tune with all that is best both theologically and psychologically in our rich Catholic tradition. The following points should be noted:

1. Celtic spirituality is very sacramental. The sacramental perspective sees the divine in the human, the infinite in the finite, the eternal in the historical. The Anglican scholar, Archbishop Temple, pointed out that Christianity is the most avowedly materialistic of all the great religions. Our faith is grounded in the mystery of the Incarnation. The Word became flesh and dwelt among us. The physical reality of Jesus Christ expresses the absolute sign of God in our world, the

foundational sacrament of Christianity. It was easy for the Celts to understand how God's healing, nourishing, cleansing power is mediated through water, oil, bread, touch and the laying on of hands.

2. In our Celtic perspective God is at the heart of all creation and we can recognise His presence in situations and relationships. Nature is not just a sign of God's presence but the medium through which God speaks to us. The poet Patrick Kavanagh reflects this in much of his work, *"men build their dreams as they build their circle of friends. God is in the bits and pieces of everyday, a kiss here and a laugh there and sometimes tears; a pearl necklace around the neck of poverty."* (from The Great Hunger)

   The nearness of God is illustrated by the well-known St. Patrick's Breastplate.

   I bind unto myself today, The strong name of the Trinity,
   By invocation of the same, the Three in One and One in Three.
   I bind unto myself today, the power of God to hold and lead,
   His eye to watch, His might to stay, His ear to hearken to my need.

3. The Communion of Saints is easily understood as there is a strong bond between us and the people who have gone before us. The pictures of our favourite saints, once so common in Irish homes, St. Patrick, St. Brigit, St. Theresa, St. Padre Pio, and others are simple reminders of people who are close to us, with whom we can have an easy familiarity, like photos of family friends.

4. This leads to a very realistic approach to the mystery of death because time merges into eternity. Time is not a straight line but a circle to be completed.

   The old Irish wake was considered by many psychologists as the best way to face the great mystery of death. There is the social gathering with some refreshments, the recalling of memories, often telling humorous stories, the collective support and sympathy, the prayers and the farewell. It is facing reality within the context of our Christian faith in the resurrection. What is death but the blowing out of the candle because the dawn has arrived.

5. Here are a few more points about Celtic Christian spirituality. It is an exultant spirituality. We badly need to celebrate our religion. We have a history of obligation rather than celebration. It also accepts the reality of suffering and death. The great High Crosses that we have were symbols of the victory of Christ over death, of good over evil. So important today in times of pessimism.

6. The wholeness approach of the Celts to the human body should encourage a healthy approach to human sexuality which is so necessary in today's world.

   The two extremes to be avoided are the rigid Janenism of the past that influenced a lot of Church teaching and the rampant permissiveness of today's society when anything goes. The former looked upon sex with grave suspicion as an occasion of sin, rather than as a life giving force, a gift of God. The latter abuses this gift for selfish reasons making it a consumer product, bought and sold. Think of the dreadful pornography industry of today and the traffic in sex slaves.

7. Celtic Christian spirituality means being close to God the Father through Jesus In the power of the Holy Spirit. The Word became flesh and lived among us. The poet Joseph Mary Plunkett captures this in one of the most beautiful poems in the English language. I have quoted it in my other book but it is worth quoting again. It is called **The Presence of God.**

I see his blood upon the rose
And in the stars the glory of His eyes.
His body gleams amid eternal snows
His tears fall from the skies.

I see His face in every flower,
The thunder and the singing of the birds
Are but His voice and carven by His power
Rocks are His written words.

All pathways by His feet are worn,
His strong heart stirs the ever-beating sea.
His crown of thorns is twined with every thorn.
His cross is every tree.

Chapter Twenty-eight

Don't Give up

My faith in a personal God and in Jesus Christ, our Saviour, is not so much an air-raid shelter in times of trouble but more of a launching pad into the unknown and the dark. If I'm a sort of salesman for God then I prefer to sell courage rather than insurance, courage to face the reality of life with honesty and integrity. We need that courage today as we face a lot of uncertainties. I took on writing these few pieces as a sort of occupational therapy at the beginning of that dreadful pandemic last year. It is still with us. We are now in January 2021 and we face an uncertain future with a lot of difficulties, but we must never give up. I love this little piece which I got from St. Patrick's magazine a long time ago: It's called: ***Don't give up.***

When things go wrong as they sometimes will,
When the road you're treading seems all uphill,
When the funds are low and the debts are high,
And you want to smile but you have to sigh.
When care is pressing you down a bit,
Rest if you must but don't you quit.

Life is queer with its twists and turns
As every one of us sometimes learns,
And many a failure turns about,
When he might have won had he stuck it out.
Don't give up though the pace seems slow.
You may succeed with another blow.

Success is failure turned inside out,
The silver tint of the cloud of doubt,
And you never can tell how close you are,
It may be near when it seems so far.
So stick to the fight when you're hardest hit,
It's when things seem worst that you must not quit.

The last year has been a tough one for me. I spent over a week in hospital. I lost a bit of my ear, skin cancer. My legs are weak and I need a trolley to help me walk around. So my days of driving, the game of golf, even shopping trips are now but happy memories. And the corona virus casts a dark shadow. Still I shouldn't complain. We are very well looked after here in our retirement house in Rathgar. We have Mass in our chapel every morning, so every day I thank God for all his blessings. This year I reach 90 and if I don't reach it, I'll send you all a card from the pearly gates, if I reach them!

Let me finish with a brief reflection on a beautiful Feast, that of **the Sacred Heart of Jesus.**

We celebrate this beautiful Feast in June and we are challenged to think what it means to us.

There is no feast in honour of the Sacred Brain although we know that the brain is the centre of all intelligence. But the Sacred Heart symbolises God's love for us made visible in Jesus. This love is poured out for us in a thousand different ways, ultimately by Jesus' death on the Cross for our salvation.

As Christians our spiritual lives are founded on our relationship with Jesus. He is God's Word of love to us. He is our word of love back to the Father. Jesus is God's fingerprints on our human flesh. He is our anam-cara, our soul friend. He once told his disciples, *"I call you friends,"* so we can talk to Jesus as our friend and share our hopes and fears, our worries and complaints with him.

The love of God for us symbolised by the Sacred Heart must be revealed by us in our daily lives by our love for others. It is expressed in a thousand different ways, by caring, sharing, forgiving and helping. Mercy and kindness are at the heart of the Christian Gospel. Love lights up the world and makes it beautiful. The absence of love means darkness and despair.

The night has a thousand eyes, the day but one.
But the light of the whole world dies with the setting sun.
The mind has a thousand eyes, the heart but one.
But the light of the whole world dies when love is done.

A bell is not a bell until you ring it.
A song is not a song until you sing it.
Love was not put into our hearts to stay.
Love is not love until you give it away.